To my friend
hope you will enjoy "

John

Elks do not Speak English

John Murolo

authorHOUSE®

AuthorHouse™ UK Ltd.
500 Avebury Boulevard
Central Milton Keynes, MK9 2BE
www.authorhouse.co.uk
Phone: 08001974150

Published by AuthorHouse 03/15/2012

ISBN: 978-1-4520-0983-4 (sc)
ISBN: 978-1-4520-0984-1 (dj)
ISBN: 978-1-4678-9426-5 (e)

Synopsis

The book has been written to describe our experiences of fifteen years in Finland and to give a little taste of this country to people who do not know it.

It is not a view from a short-time visitor. It stems from a love and affection that has developed from spending half a year in Finland for a long time, through beautiful summers and very harsh winters, living in a small community where the sense of its past prevails.

The purpose of the book is to make Finland better known and appreciated by the world at large, but more importantly, to have the Finns understand themselves and their country, overcoming their fundamental shyness towards foreigners that exists despite their technical achievements in modern society and the general respect they enjoy as a nation on the global scene.

This is not a travel book. It is simply an analysis of the character and habits of the Finns and an attempt to capture in words the natural beauty of a land at the edge of the world

Acknowledgements

This book was written by one person, but it is about the Finnish experiences of both my wife and me during the many years we have spent in this beautiful country.

Many good friends contributed to this book. Some did it unknowingly, simply by being our friends; others did it deliberately to broaden our understanding of their country and to help me write things that were factual and correct.

The list of names would be too long and probably boring to the reader, but I am sure all my friends will know that I am remembering them.

One special debt of gratitude has to be for my wife, who accepted to spend many lonely evenings, often falling asleep in front of the television, while I was in my little room, sitting at the laptop, writing. She has been patient and supportive, at times giving me ideas and reminding me of many episodes that I had forgotten.

The book has to be dedicated to her.

Preface

Finland is an unknown country.

Most people know that it is somewhere up there, in the north, near Russia. A lot of people confuse it with Iceland. Many people seem to know about Finnish mosquitos and reindeer. And, of course, the majority of children under ten know that it is the homeland of Father Christmas and of the Moomies, the amusing little creatures that have captured the imagination of children the world over. They were created by Tove Jansson, a solitary lady who lived in a remote small island deep in the Gulf of Finland. But that is about it. After all, by definition "Finland" means "The End of the Land".

This book intends to present Finland to the uninitiated, with an insight into the culture, habits, and peculiarities of this naturally beautiful country and of its small and charming population who seem to live two distinct and separate lives, one in summer and one in winter.

After some fourteen years spending wonderful long spells by the shores of one of the major lakes in the heart of Finland, Celia and I consider ourselves a fully-fledged part of the Finnish habitat and completely integrated into the rural society that represents the backbone of the country's long history and of the nation's short history.

Our love for Finland has convinced me to write this book in order to offer an objective view of a country made almost more of water than of land, where the millennial power and magic of the forests are still the dominant factors in shaping its inhabitants' character and where the ruin towards which our poor old world is racing still seems remote and almost impossible.

Recently I came across an old map of Northern Europe, dating back to 1486. The outline of countries like Britain, Denmark, Norway, and Sweden, as well as what were to become the Baltic States, could just about be identified. Finland was not there. Only six years later, Columbus would complete his epic voyage from the Spanish port of Palos to discover the new continent so far away, and yet by the end of the fifteenth century Finland had still not been found by the Geographer.

The explorers probably felt that beyond the Winter freeze of the North Sea and the land of Sweden, so clearly visible from the shores of northern Demark and from the walls of Hamlet's Elsinore Castle, the world ended, engulfed in the mists and shadows of perennially icy forests.

Even today the country maintains a mysterious face that makes it little understood and scarcely known to the rest of the globe. I hope that this book will succeed in revealing some of its attractions and will help a little in giving the Finns the confidence and the belief they need and in making them appreciate how lucky they are to live in one of the few remaining corners of the world where, despite an advanced modern technology culture, so far society has managed to keep a very clean face and a good dose of common sense.

Maybe with this book I shall succeed in convincing the Finns that their evident shyness towards the rest of the world and their anxiety about being accepted as a complete and progressive society are unfounded. The fundamental honesty of the nation – after all, it was the first to repay in full the debt to the Americans after the World War II – and its scientific and technical achievements over the past forty years make it one of the most modern and respected in the world.

As long as they manage to hold on to their forests for many years to come!

Introduction

Tuomo and Paula, two good friends of ours, picked us up from our home at around eleven at night. It was December 28, and like everyone else, we were still looking for things that might somehow prolong the Christmas holiday feeling, which always seems to disappear as soon as the day itself has gone and all the preparations have been consumed, either in success or disaster, leaving a sad sense of emptiness.

The snow was still falling heavily, with large puffy flakes, as it had been for the whole day, and the old red Volvo was purring quietly along the lane by the cemetery, where hundreds of candles were still flickering on every grave, reminders of the long-standing Christmas Eve tradition of visiting the loved ones who have passed away.

The studded tyres were gripping the compact snow with a muffled grinding noise. The temperature had plunged to twenty below, and the old theory – so common in Mediterranean countries - that it cannot snow when it is below freezing was proving completely wrong. The car was warm, and we were all in a jovial mood.

We had dressed up accordingly, with all-in-one ski suits, woollen hats, and gloves, and for some reason I had even thought of putting a sharp hunter's knife in my pocket. It was no doubt completely unnecessary, but it seemed to me that an outing into the Finnish forest, especially at this time of night in the middle of winter, required the rather childish feeling of safety that the small knife was giving me.

I had even bought a larger one in Helsinki on our very first visit to Finland, where we had decided to spend a weekend over New Year's Eve some years earlier. The shop was full of Finnish objects, some genuine and some certainly made in the Far East, and knives were prominent. They were really made in Finland, and they looked impressive and very sharp.

At the time it was still possible to carry a knife in the suitcase across borders without being arrested and incarcerated, and so I took the knife back to England as a souvenir from this country. It is still in my wardrobe in its leather pouch, having never been used. It just brings back nice memories. I do not believe that I would have the time or the inclination to try to use it, even if a burglar should decide to visit us in the middle of the night. All the same it looks both dangerous and comforting.

Celia had prepared a carrier bag with some sausages, mustard, and bread, and we had our torches. I could not help feeling a bit crazy and wondering whether midnight in December should be considered a normal time for a picnic in a Finnish forest. But, as they say, "When in Finland . . ." Or was that Rome?

Tuomo drove for about twenty minutes along the deserted country road that ran along one side of the South Lake. Dim spots of brightness showed occasionally amidst the dark trees like small signs of life in an otherwise empty black and white scenery, cut by the car lights over the pale blue-grey ribbon of the road. The snow seemed to come upon us at speed in waves of thick flakes, almost circling around the car as if pushed through an invisible wind tunnel.

Our friends had offered to take us out for the evening and show us a bit of Finland that was still new to us, despite the fact that we had already spent some five winters in this country. A lot of it was still surprising us. When Paula told us that they would come for us at eleven at night, we had no idea what to expect. We were just a little amused at having to dress up when we would normally go to bed. She said that she would bring some coffee.

We did not dare risk being late; we had learnt that it is just not done in Finland, so we were ready well before eleven o'clock, and by the time the car stopped in our drive, we were beginning to melt under our padded clothes. Never in any of the several countries we had visited or lived in had we encountered a more precise and punctual race. When it comes to time, Finns do not compromise; they make a mental note of the hour and the minute, and they stick to it with religious accuracy. I can only imagine the potential confusion in a Finn's mind over a formula used very frequently in English dinner invitations – "7.30 for 8.00". What does it mean? Is it 7.30 or 8.00? What if I arrive at 7.45? What happens between 7.30 and 8.00?

When we lived in Italy, if we invited friends for drinks or dinner, we could comfortably start running our bath at the time our guests were supposed to arrive, as we knew full well that they would be at least an hour late. In Italy it is de rigeur. In Finland it is practically against the law, and punctuality suits us well. In Mediterranean countries, punctuality is an incomprehensible imposition.

The snow was still falling when Tuomo parked the car in a small lay-by. Out of the car boot came the rucksacks and our bags with sausages, bread, coffee, and various other accessories that are always useful for a picnic, and soon we were following Tuomo along the road. The heavy snow was bending tree branches, and the small light of our torches was playing with the flakes and making strange-looking shadows on either side of the road, where every tree for a second became a creature out of a northern winter tale.

Tuomo was leading at a fast pace, seemingly knowing where he was heading. Then he took a sharp turn over the bank of ploughed snow off the road and into the forest. He looked like a man on a mission. We had not seen any sign pointing anywhere. Everything was dark and quiet. Everything looked the same, with that sameness that only snow can give to all things. And yet Tuomo knew where we had to go.

Walking in deep snow was difficult. The road had been the easy part. Now we were knee-deep on uneven ground, and we did not want to lose sight of our leader in case we might become lost forever in that silent world of an unknown forest in the middle of winter in Finland. We were trying to put our feet into Tuomo's and Paula's prints, but even that was not easy. Everyone seems to have legs of different lengths and feet of different angles, and by making an effort to adjust our steps to the others' we risked falling over several times.

The numerous prints left by animals in the snow were also a cause of concern for us. Some looked very large and were not just the shape of a hare's trail. (These were the only ones we knew well, because we regularly had Mr Hare visiting our garden at night.) However, our friends did not seem at all bothered. I was gripping the knife handle in my pocket, stupidly feeling safer with that.

We finally came to a small opening among the trees. A small log hut became visible in the light of our torches. It looked solid, with a large opening at the front and a floor well above the ground. It was facing a circle of stones with an iron barbeque frame in the middle, and some tree trunks lay on the ground as legless benches. It all looked surreal.

After unpacking our rucksacks, Celia and Paula sat on the wooden floor of the hut, their feet dangling above the snow like children sitting on chairs that were too high for them. Meanwhile Tuomo walked away into the darkness to a smaller hut, where to our amazement some chopped wood had been neatly stacked. The torch light revealed also that an axe had been left so that more wood could be chopped if needed. There were no warning signs, no notices that axes may be dangerous, no cut-off limbs left as evidence of danger, just a simple axe to chop wood. Nothing more, nothing less.

People are supposed to know what an axe is for without written instructions. Images of accidents and compensation claims came to our distorted minds, but we were in Finland, where human brains obviously still had some intelligence and common sense left in them. The axe was left for everyone to use freely.

By the wood shed another small hut was visible. It was the loo. As rudimentary as it might be, it was a loo – yes, a loo in the middle of a forest.

It seemed to us as if Paula and Tuomo had actually booked the place for our picnic. Wooden spears leant against the side of the shelter, slightly blackened by frequent use over the fire and by the sausages that they had held. There was a visitors' book neatly placed in a pouch on the wall. People had been there before us from Estonia, Lapland, Canada, and other places.

Our friends explained that such huts are common places in the Finnish forests. They are maintained by local councils for the purpose of offering a shelter to travellers, a welcome rest to skiers, an outing for families, and a midnight picnic site for crazy visitors. The hut floors are always well above ground for insulation purposes and for safety. The location of these places is well marked on maps, and this shows the importance and the influence that forests have on Finns' life.

After piling some wood between the stones, Tuomo lit the fire. The glow soon spread some light around us. Our sausages tasted wonderful, and the coffee was very warming. We spent the next two hours sitting around the fire, talking and laughing in the minus 20 degrees temperature. The thought of madness came to us a few times, but if madness it was, it was the best form of madness. In fact, it was nature at its best. We did not feel cold, and we did not feel scared. We felt as if we now belonged to a very privileged world.

By the time we were dropped back at home, we were rather tired, but we sat up for a while, talking about the evening while sipping some well-deserved whisky. Paula and Tuomo were good friends, and in their simple way they had shown us Finland.

Helsinki

Some years ago we decided to spend some of our weekends visiting European capital cities where we had never had the opportunity or the reason to stay. So often people tend to fly to exotic places on the other side of the world, and they neglect what they have on their own doorstep. Europe is small enough to allow weekend breaks almost anywhere, and we had been to a number of cities, the last of which had been Copenhagen a few weeks earlier.

So we booked a hotel in Helsinki. We knew very little of Finland, and the only association we could claim with this country was that Celia had known a Finnish au pair who had looked after friends' children many years ago and that I had an uncle who had ended up refereeing fencing matches at the Helsinki Olympics in 1952.

Finland had always seemed to be at the end of the world, a remote cold country squeezed against its neighbouring Russia, famous only for its reindeer and Santa Claus and the colourful costumes of its most northern inhabitants. We were curious about it.

The little booklet we bought prior to leaving London told us that the currency was the Markka, that coffee was the national drink, and that saunas were the Finns' most common occupation. That was not a lot to go on.

John Murolo

We arrived at Vantaa airport in mid-afternoon on December 30. The light was fading fast, and during the short trip into the city on the courtesy coach, we tried to take in and absorb every detail – the lights that occasionally showed through the trees as small golden dots escaping from the black shadows of houses immersed in woods and the illegible words on signposts along the road. This was a very different country. Snow was on the ground, and everything had the kind of soft cotton-wool appearance of a postcard from the North Pole.

The Vakuuna Hotel – I believe the name has since changed – was imposing and badly lit, with a cavernous lobby in which some scattered brown leather armchairs did not quite give a warm welcome to visitors. A few people were sitting in silence, like in a railway station waiting room. I remember asking at the desk for some help with the luggage, and the lady at the reception, after raising her eyebrows in surprise, came herself with a wheeled trolley to carry our cases into the hotel. I felt embarrassed.

When I had arranged the booking from England by telephone, I was asked whether we would prefer a room with a waterbed or with a sauna. I was a bit puzzled by the question but opted for the latter. I was not sure if a waterbed would turn out to be something of an erotic experiment or a way to be seasick; we had never slept in one. We had never had a sauna either, but it seemed a more interesting adventure. The lady at the other end of the line was very courteous and helpful and spoke impeccable English.

It was the end of 1993, and we were going to spend New Years' Eve in Helsinki.

Right from the start we liked Helsinki. After a walk along the Esplanade, we decided to have dinner in a place that we found on a corner in a side street. The name of the restaurant was Richard's. We have recently found out that it has since been turned into a very fashionable and famous French restaurant by the name of Chez Dominique. Richard's was a rather narrow and long restaurant at the time, and it was possible to see the chefs in action behind the long counter of the bar. The staff made us immediately welcome, making every effort to speak in English and to find us an English menu. We had a simple but excellent dinner, following the young waitress' suggestion of fish in breadcrumbs and garlic potatoes.

We went back to Richard's a few years later when we spent a night in Helsinki as a break from our country home in central Finland, and we were very pleased to find that the food was still excellent. Nowadays, you have to book well in advance to secure a table, and I am told that the food is of a very high standard. We have not tried it as yet.

I remember strolling along the Esplanade in daylight the following morning and admiring the beautiful shops on the northern side, the lovely buildings, the coffee places, the huge Stockmann bookshop, and the market in the harbour with such a variety of fish and vegetables and woollen gloves. It was all neat and tidy, and the people were kind.

It was New Year's Eve, so in the evening we went to Senate Square and stood squashed in the middle of a crazy young crowd, amazed at how the rockets were being lit among people, seemingly with complete disregard for safety. We had visions of eyes being burnt, hair on fire, fingers lost, and clothes smouldering. A few policemen were walking among the crowd, but they did not appear too concerned. We stood there like thousands of other onlookers from almost every corner of the world, enjoying the madness of this Nordic and supposedly unemotional country celebrating the end of a year.

We walked the short distance from Senate Square to Amadeus, a beautiful restaurant run by ladies, where we had our New Year's Eve dinner of delicious dishes of fish, elk meat, and mushrooms. Amadeus has long since closed down, and in its place is now a Mexican diner. We have not been back. Helsinki has lost an excellent culinary example.

Somehow we felt comfortable and almost at home, as if an invisible link had existed in our previous life with this land and with these people.

Helsinki is a relatively small city. The central area is tiny and is easily covered on foot. From the harbour market, with its imposing Orthodox Church in the background, to the Olympic Stadium is no more than a forty-minute walk. And that is the beauty of the city. It still has a human dimension, like one of the many "villages" making up London. In Piccadilly you are a nonentity, but in Notting Hill

High Street or Camden Market or by the Thames in Chiswick you can still feel an individual. In Helsinki you always feel human.

I shall never forget the expression on the hotel concierge's face when the following day we asked for suggestions on the best way for us to see the famous lakes. "But they are frozen," he pointed out with a smile. "You will not see them." All the same he suggested we take the train to Tampere, the second largest city. (The inhabitants of Turku, the old capital city, would disagree with this, claiming that their city is the second largest. Having seen both, I am afraid I have to sustain the first theory, even if this will make me quite unpopular in Turku). The train journey would take about one and a half hours, and we would be able to see some of the country, albeit all covered in snow.

The station was right opposite the hotel, so it was easy to make a decision. The enormous statues of the four semi-naked men adorning the building are the landmark of Helsinki train station. The station was the creation of the famous architect Saarinen, and it is in complete contrast with the ugly box-like building on the opposite side of the square that is lit up at night by an array of advertising slogans and company names. The station belongs to the category of imposing and architecturally striking buildings that can be found in many cities round the world. Often train stations are ugly and uninteresting constructions or are irrationally squeezed between apartment blocks. Rarely do they attract a second look from the passers-by or from the travellers departing and arriving.

Helsinki train station may not be beautiful, but it certainly is imposing, and the sight of it remains in your mind, as does St Pancras in London or the Central Station in Milan. The interior is the same as any other large railway station in the western world. The main hall, with its constant buzzing of people of all kinds, carrying all imaginable luggage, arriving, departing, saying goodbyes and welcomes, is the usual impersonal and draughty room you find in New York, London, or Paris, or even Glasgow or Koln. In a train station people always seem to be in a hurry. In an airport people in a hurry are the exception, and they are always frowned upon, because they are generally the ones holding the plane back and making it miss its departing slot. Nobody seems to take it easy in a train station, and everything seems messy. Helsinki station was no exception.

We travelled to Tampere. The train left punctually (well, of course, we were in Finland). It was clean and warm and it arrived on time. With our noses against the window we saw a lot of snow, and we thought we saw some lakes too, also covered in snow. They were difficult to distinguish from empty fields, and only when solitary figures appeared, hunched over a fishing hole, could we be sure that they were actually lakes.

We spent a pleasant day in Tampere, and when we returned at the station for our journey back to Helsinki, a loudspeaker announced that unfortunately the train would be some twenty minutes late. Waiting passengers seemed rather horrified at the delay. After all, the train was only coming from Lapland – some thousand kilometres north! In midwinter! When it appeared and finally stopped by the platform, solid ice was covering its front, and the doors had to be warmed before they could be opened. They were frozen. A twenty-minute delay seemed to us very reasonable.

We were back in our room with ample time to relax and then have dinner in another good restaurant called Konig, just a few hundred metres from the hotel. It had been a good day, and by its end we had made the decision that we wanted a house in the Finnish countryside. The hotel concierge's suggestion had been an excellent one.

We have been back to Helsinki many times since that first weekend, and on a couple of occasions we have stayed at the same Vakuuna Hotel. It has since changed its name to the Sokos Hotel, part of the Sokos conglomerate of supermarkets, hotels, and department stores. The last time was in August a few years ago during a very hot and humid spell, when the wind from the south-west brought unusually heavy and stifling air. We had decided to travel by coach from our village so as not to worry about parking or having to drive in unknown one-way systems. The coach had been comfortably air-conditioned and surprisingly inexpensive, and when we arrived at the hotel we were ready for a relaxing drink in our large room on the top floor, with access to the roof terrace.

Unfortunately the temperature in the room, added to the sun beating on the large windows that took up the whole of one wall, made the place unbearable. There was no air conditioning, we were told when I called the reception desk in desperation; the place was too old to install a cooling system, and we would have to bear the heat. But, Finland being Finland and Finns being Finns, a young lady soon arrived with two large standing electrical fans and profusely apologised for the inconvenience. We had no heart to moan further about the room temperature. We walked out on the terrace overlooking the main square, carrying our drinks, and we sat in the only bit of space that we could find in the shade. The hot August breeze seemed a little cooler on that rooftop, and the noise of the traffic in the square down below reached us muffled by the distance. We were pleased to be in Helsinki again.

Many years and many visits later we still enjoy the city, with its permanent holiday air and its relaxed atmosphere. We often watch people stroll to work in the morning among the gardens of the Esplanade, holding their briefcases, some in so-called business suits. (I always wondered who invented this expression. Is a business suit a kind of dark uniform that has the power of making people feel important, or is it a kind of class identification emblem that is supposed to distinguish one particular category of worker from plumbers, decorators, carpenters, or bricklayers who have their own business but have no desk or padded chair or seat on the commuters' train?) Everyone walks erect and stiff in Finland, almost as if in a well-rehearsed march, with a wonderful posture that gives girls incredibly appealing figures and men incredibly severe looks.

Helsinki is a casual city with plenty of young people, as well as an elegant city. Some of the stores along and around the Esplanade nowadays have nothing to envy to Milan, London, Paris, and New York, and in the evening the city's countless restaurants, bars, clubs, and coffee places come alive. In summer the tables sprawl onto pavements and walkways, painting the streets with myriads of colours and noises in the perennial light of the northern sun, which for a couple of months between June and August never disappears. In Winter the windows are steamed up by the human warmth that clashes through the glass with the sub-zero temperatures outside, giving a cloudy and ghostly appearance to the figures inside, in the perennial darkness of the northern days, when the few hours of dim light are easily pushed away by long lasting nights. It is still a human city.

The famous market in the pebbled harbour at the end of the beautiful Esplanade, where smoked fish can still be eaten by the stalls and crocheted colourful hats hang by the dozen from wooden hooks, has now become a little byzantine. Chinese and Korean-made products are sold as authentic Finnish artefacts to hordes of Japanese and Chinese tourists who are under the strange belief that they will take back to their countries true examples of Finnish craft. We do not feel that we are tourists – in fact, we are not – and we cannot but smile at the changes that the city has undergone in a matter of a few years.

The character of the Esplanade on a warm sunny summer day is unique. By 7.30 in the morning, people are walking along the dusty pedestrian central area or sitting on the wooden benches that face the fresh sun shining from the harbour's end. Blond pony-tailed girls in sleeveless tops and working trousers rake the whole place, almost in slow motion, collecting the remains of the previous day, when crowds of young people sprawled on the grass enjoying a chat and a drink (or two).

It is amusing that in other parts of the city the local Council seems to give that very same job to old pensioners with big beer bellies and leaves the Esplanade in charge of lovely young things who appear to fit in well with the hundreds of passers-by with their immensely long legs and slim bodies, all with flowing blonde hair and a self-assured posture. Nowhere in the world have I seen such a collection of sun-tanned young female examples of fresh uninhibited confidence as along Helsinki's Esplanade on a summer afternoon.

The Home Indoor Market still stands in a beautifully Victorian red-brick building right by the sea, where families of swans swim in the murky oily water, hoping for some food from visitors. Its wooden shops are elaborate and old-fashioned, selling smoked reindeer and elk meat, smoked fish, and vegetables. Most also sell French and Italian cheeses and Middle Eastern condiments that have nothing to do with Finland. Unfortunately, the selection of products goes with the demand, and Helsinki is now as international as any major world city. Its unique identity is rapidly disappearing.

Luckily, pockets of traditional culture may still be found, especially in the "design and antique district", a short distance from the top end of the Esplanade. Lovely antique shops and art dealers still sell original old Finnish, Swedish, and Russian works. Nothing is from the Far East … yet.

House Hunting

We flew back to England with our minds still on the emptiness of a snow-covered country, on the cleanliness of the air that had hit us as soon we had stepped out of Vantaa airport, and on the kindness of the people we had met.

London airport is a shock to the system at the best of times. Returning from the peace of Finland, it is a horror scene. We were again anonymous, in a crowd of thousands of other anonymous people of a thousand races, pushing our way on the left-hand side of the moving conveyor towards passport control and the luggage hall, struggling to keep up with the pace of the others in order to arrive in the luggage hall before the conveyor belt would make our suitcases disappear again into the inaccessible bowels of the airport.

I have always wondered why we still have the compulsion to walk on those flat escalators that have been fitted to help travellers walk less. We all do it, and we always enjoy the sense of satisfaction in moving faster than others walking on firm ground. We look at them as we pass them, almost with an attitude of superiority like mannequins fixed to a magic tape coming from somewhere and going nowhere.

The air outside the airport was as warm and polluted, as ever. A hood of smells and fumes came over our head, pressing down on us and squeezing our necks. The trolley did not seem to follow our orders; one lift was not working; the person in front of us was stuck, with his luggage wedged between the walls of the extremely tight passage that leads to the car park and that makes me curse its designer every time. Finland seemed again a distant and remote country, and we missed it.

It proved easy to have a small advertisement placed in the Helsinki Sanomat. The young lady on the phone was most helpful with useful suggestions, and the English text would be translated into Finnish by the newspaper's staff at no cost. We wanted to find a house by a lake somewhere in the country for two or three years.

We had a good number of replies, all collected in Helsinki and sent to us in England, each one with some photos of the building, the garden, and the lake. They were from different parts of Finland, completely unknown places to us, and we needed a map of the country to get an idea of the locations. I remember one from Kuopio (that looked very far from anywhere), another on the south coast, and a nice-looking house in another place with a name that was unbelievably impossible to pronounce or remember

They all looked pleasant and colourful, with wooden walls, pretty white windows and polished boarded floors covered by scattered rugs. One of the replies was written in excellent English and described the house in detail. It enclosed some photos of a dark log house, on one level, with a garden surrounding it. We could see some flower beds, a lot of hostas with their large fat leaves, a lake edge not far away, and a lady bending over some wild roses. Something about the place caught our imagination. It was in central Finland on the western side of Lake Paijanne that on the map looked long and thin, right in the middle of the pear-shaped tummy of the country.

We wanted to see it for real, and Celia immediately felt that our search was over.

It was May when we flew to Helsinki again, after arranging to go and view the house by Paijanne. We spent another weekend in Helsinki, staying once more at the Vakuuna hotel opposite the station. I do not believe that the staff remembered us at all, but we liked to think that they did when again they proved to be most helpful and obliging. We had a room with a sauna, and we pretended to know by now all the secrets and traditions connected with it. After all, we had done it before (once). A full chapter later on is dedicated to this most important Finnish occupation.

We also tried to find something in the travel leaflets available in the hotel about the village we would be driving to on the following morning. Its name looked very small on the map, especially if compared to places like Turku, Tampere, Oulu, Kuopio and others that did not quite register with us. It appeared to be on a straight line going north from Helsinki, about halfway along the side of Lake Paijanne.

It may have been the untold excitement or the loud noise of the traffic in the street below, mixed with the regular clanging of trams, until the small hours. The fact is that we did not sleep much, and in the morning as we were leaving the hotel for the hire-car office, we mentioned to the concierge that our room was obviously on the wrong side of the building and that we had been kept awake for most of the night by the Friday crowds celebrating the end of yet another working week. The double or treble glazing, so efficient in protecting from the cold weather, did not seem to work against noise.

The gentleman at the hotel desk was most sympathetic and assured us that during our absence all our things would be moved to another wing. Sure enough, by the time we returned in the evening, everything had been transferred with meticulous precision to the quieter side of the hotel. That night we had a wonderful restful sleep. The Vakuuna was still badly lit and cavernous, but the staff were always excellent.

We drove for over two hours in the hired Volvo, trying to remember the instructions from the Hertz man on how to get onto the E75 (as it was then called) heading north. We followed the Mannerheimintie – one of the longest city avenues in the world – before turning right by the small and beautiful lake overlooked by the Opera House. We saw the beautiful design of Finlandia House on our right and the tired old-fashioned structure of the 1952 Olympic Stadium on our left. Then the city centre turned into the ugly square apartment blocks that are the heritage of suburban town architecture of the Fifties and Sixties anywhere in continental Europe, particularly in countries that directly or indirectly had to live through the Russian influence. There was street after street of grey boxes, often looking rather neglected and tired, with their plaster occasionally peeling off and with their postage-stamp size gardens left to the invasion of weeds.

Slowly, as we progressed on our journey, the country took over.

It was spring and the trees were green – the fresh and luscious tone of green that so quickly disappears as soon as June arrives. Nature was enjoying once again the feast of colours after the mostly monochrome winter. It was a very different kind of spring. We had left Heathrow the previous day on a warm and sunny morning, with the oaks out in full and the field covered in tall grass, almost ready for the first hay cut. Daffodils had long been forgotten, and lawns had been mowed since February. Here Spring was in the air and on the calendar, but it seemed as if nature had not caught on to the idea yet. The fields were neatly ploughed, but only a delicate hint of green shoots was visible on the dark rich earth.

The landscape was gentle and undulating, dotted by the occasional red and white wooden house amidst a cluster of trees. Each house was surrounded by an array of wooden huts that seemed planted with no order, as if erected on the spur of the moment whenever the need occurred for extra storage. The houses had no hedges or fences or boundaries, and their land seemed to merge with the fields and the forest. Their gardens seemed to be the whole of Finland.

The traffic was light, with large distances between cars, all moving with an air of relaxation. It was a Saturday morning, and most of the people wishing to spend their weekend in the country had left the city on the previous evening after work.

Celia and I made the inevitable comparison with the few miles that we had covered along the M4 on our way to Heathrow airport. We had left home rather early, despite the fact that our flight would not leave until mid-morning. We knew well how temperamental the traffic could be on that particular motorway that is claimed to be the busiest in the world. Many times it had taken us over an hour at a ridiculously slow pace to drive the short distance, with the result that Celia had become anxious and had palpitations by the time we reached the terminal. So we had allowed ourselves plenty of time.

Proceeding north along the E75 – as it used to be called – we recognised some of the names of the places we had noticed the night before when in the hotel we had worked out our route on a map – Jarvenpaa, Hollola, Lahti …

Someone somewhere had told us that Lahti is comparable to Croydon in England. Busy and known for its furniture manufacturing and for its skiing facilities, Lahti is a major city, after Helsinki, Tampere, and Turku. Its name on the map was written in thick letters. Somehow the comparison with Croydon discouraged us from visiting it for many years. Croydon has now been incorporated in the Greater London. It is overcrowded, overnoisy, overpolluted, and mostly famous for the presence of Lunar House, the Immigration Centre, the point of arrival into the English system for so many thousands of hopefuls from all over the world.

Approaching Lahti, we could see in the distance on our left the three tall ramps for ski-jumping competitions on which many a world cup has been held. Three different heights, like a family of long-legged concrete monsters overlooking the town. Several square white blocks of flats emerged from the tree tops, and small industrial estates stood beside the road, with the usual low flat-roof buildings.

We turned off the motorway that would continue to Mikkeli and left "Croydon" behind. The road became a single carriageway, and the lakes began to appear, clear deep blue spots of water surrounded by forests. Central Finland almost has more lakes than population, and this time we could see them at last. They were not frozen or covered in snow. The trees, in their spring awakening, were not yet fully covered in leaves, and it was still possible to notice the lakes through them. They seemed to be everywhere.

The more we progressed north, the emptier the road became, until our car was the only one left and we could better admire the peaceful countryside, dotted occasionally with the red and white wooden houses that looked isolated and tranquil, their colourful mailboxes lined up like small soldiers at the top of the lanes leading to them.

We saw a few cows, peacefully carrying their horns on the fresh spring grass, their udders strapped with belts tied to their back to support the heavy burden of milk.

We had received very precise directions in English, written to us by the house proprietor's daughter, and after almost two hours we turned off the main road towards the village centre. The road was dug up and uneven. It was being completely resurfaced, and large rough pebbles had been laid as the base for the tarmac, but nothing would be finished until after the winter freeze had settled the sand and the gravel. For many months people would drive on an uncomfortable and noisy surface, excellent for ruining car suspensions and tyres. On the other hand, the alternative would be to have to do the same job again every year, the tarmac easily cracking if laid on a base that has not been well solidified because of sub-zero temperatures.

It was May and winter seemed so far away. In fact, winter can disappear very quickly, and it can also come round the corner very quickly as soon as August is over. When the Ruska time arrives in September, with its feast of autumn colours, winter is close. Temperatures begin to drop, and daylight fades earlier. Wood is piled up ready for the welcoming fires, for oven baking, and for saunas. And Ruska was only three months away.

We have since become accustomed to the regular routine of life changes between winter and summer. By the time spring arrives and joins summer, Ruska feels so distant that its wonderful colours are only vaguely still alive in our memory.

We had reached our village, our destination. In the hotel the previous evening, I had tried to learn something about the place, with its 3,000 souls in winter and three times that number in summer. I could not find a great deal of information, apart from the existence of a craft cottage industry – knives, mats, woodwork, bread – and a ferry service to the opposite side of Paijanne. The service stopped in August, like most things in the Finnish country that are related to the tourist trade. After July, summer is officially over. Children return to school. Museums, restaurants, and attractions all close, and people begin to prepare for ruska once more and for the long Winter, often disappointing those visitors who travel from countries where August is still a Summer holiday month.

We turned off the uneven main street. The instructions clearly told us to turn right at a certain bar, which apparently did not enjoy the best of reputations, and continue up to a small wooden bridge that connected the mainland with a large island. The bridge was only about ten metres long, gently arched over a small stretch of water that linked the two sides of the lake. We passed a small marina on our left, with many tiny boats moored along the wooden jetties. Across the water we could see the tall brick chimney of a paper mill, no longer in use, and a harbour with more, larger boats. The water was an intense tone of blue, gently brushed by the May breeze, and the air was pure.

The small road ran along the side of an immaculately kept cemetery and passed some wooden houses that backed on to the water edge. We tried to recognise the log house we had seen in the photographs. We could not, and we ended by going back and forth on the small road a couple of times, until a man, who was frantically waving his arms, shouted to us, "Velcom! Velcom!"

Juhani seemed friendly. He was stocky, his face lined by years of exposure to the temperament of the winter weather and to the long Summer nights of fishing on Paijanne. We exchanged a few salutations in English and in Finnish without understanding each other at all. We were lead to the house, right on the lake front.

It was a dark log house, rather long and on one floor. The garden was in fact a field where some of the grass had been cut and flower beds had been laid. There was no drive, but just the track that had been made by cars using the same patch for years. There were no hedges, but lots of trees with tall grass growing around them and invading the concrete base of the house.

Juhani's daughter Katariina was waiting for us on the doorstep, very tall and very blond. She had handwritten the letter that had been forwarded to us by the Helsinki Sanomatt in an English that was no doubt above average. She welcomed us, and we all settled around the kitchen table to talk about the house and about the terms of our possible tenancy for the next three years.

The kitchen was very spacious, and the table was round, with the rotating centre piece reminiscent of many Chinese restaurants that always tempts you to push it round and round as fast as possible, sending all glasses and cutlery off to a tangent. We always tell children off for doing it, when in fact we ourselves can never resist the temptation.

The house had been built by Juhani, with help from his son Jorma and some local friends, fifteen years earlier. It was their family home, rich with memories of Katariina growing and playing and studying. Juhani and his wife Iris had now decided to move to Spain. The harsh Finnish Winters seemed to have finally got the better of them, and they were looking forward to the move to Fuengirola, apparently an area of Spain that is popular among Finns. The choice of living in an apartment in the sun had made them decide to let the log house by Paijanne. By contrast, we had never – and still have never – been in Spain. Somehow the thought of hordes of English tourists enjoying such Spanish specialities as fish and chips and steak and kidney pie washed by warm English beer has created in our mind a limited and no doubt wrong idea of Spain. We are surely wrong in our perceptions and in our generalizations. The result is that we have always tended to go north for our breaks.

Juhani, who turned out to be sixty, declared himself tired of the snow and ice that made his bones shudder for six or seven months a year. He and Iris intended to spend the remaining years of their lives without having to worry about ice crampons, sledges, heavy Winter clothes, and the sharp northern winds that made their eyes water. Juhani was also planning to transfer the business to his son, the fishing business that his father had started almost sixty years earlier, when he had moved with his family to Central Finland from his native Karelia after this land, that was once part of the Finnish territory, had to be handed over to Russia as the outcome of the Winter Wars. Now Juhani wanted to retire.

So we sat in the kitchen around the rotating table, looking out on the lake through the incredibly large window over the worktop. The house was spacious, with lovely wooden floors and no doors between the two ends, so that the sitting room appeared immense and relaxing. On one side a series of doors led into the bedrooms, into a storage cubicle with the heating unit, into the shower room, and into the inevitable sauna. At this time baths did not seem to be a frequent feature in Finnish homes. The walls were just bare logs, and the windows had triple glazing, something we had never come across until then.

Juhani, through his daughter's interpreting, went over a few details concerning the elimination of rubbish, the functioning of the huge central heating boiler and control box, the position of the shoots over the fireplaces, the various keys, the electric panel with its array of old-fashioned fuses, the switches, and the power points. We tried to store every piece of information, but most of it escaped us soon after. Everything seemed different to what we had been used to – no painted walls, electric switches that were pressed up rather than down, a central heating system that operated with vents blowing air that had been warmed up by the water from the lake using a system of underground serpentines. It looked cumbersome and complicated, but we were told that it did work.

We were shown the garden. It was a good size plot, reduced to a rather small patch of cut grass and a couple of flower beds because of the tall weeds that had been allowed to grow around the house and by every tree or rock. The lake edge, only a few metres way, could not be seen. The grass and the reeds made a natural barrier that gave the house some privacy from passing boats but at the same time made it impossible to admire the beauty of Paijanne from the garden without having to stand on a chair.

Some ten metres from the house was another log building, smaller in size, with a little balcony at the front that overlooked a wooden jetty stretching on to the water like a floating platform, precariously connected to the land by way of a pair of wooden planks. The building – reminiscent of a gigantic doll's house – contained a sitting room, some sleeping accommodation, and a sauna, and we were told that in the Summer it was good to have saunas away from the house and closer to the lake so as to enjoy a swim after the intense heat.

Celia and I walked onto the wobbly jetty and stood looking around and across the lake. It was only a small section of the great Paijanne, winding its way through wooded peninsulas up to the village marinas. The water was inviting, with its deep crispy blue colour, fresh after the winter ice that had frozen it for several months. No other houses were visible along the lake sides, and the silence was deafening.

We liked the place.

Back in the kitchen Juhani and I shook hands, and I handed him a sterling cheque for the first three months' rent. It was as simple as that. He invited us for lunch at a local cafeteria-cum-bar. All was done.

We drove back to Helsinki pleased with our decision, and we immediately started planning our next visit, this time to our own place by the lake. We dropped the rented Volvo outside the Hertz office, and once in our hotel, we had a drink to Finland.

Everything had been terribly easy. In our enthusiasm we tried to explain to the concierge where and how far the house was, but our pronunciation of the village name must have been so very far from any resemblance of Finnish that he mistook our village for a town much further north and with an entirely different name. It was not very encouraging, but it was fun.

Homes and Gardens

We returned to our village in June, the middle of the Finnish summer, for our first stay. Juhani had built an impressive wooden fence along one side of the house to separate it from the field that belonged to his son. The archway that had been erected over the access drive resembled more the gateway to a rodeo farm in deep Texas rather than to a Finnish log house, but admittedly it gave us a certain sense of privacy, which is so important in English culture.

The fence ran the whole length of one side of the garden, from the water edge to a line of trees that marked the boundary at the back of the house. A number of strange-looking metal red boxes were set into the ground by the fence, like some kind of detectors or land mines. It was explained that these are the markers used in Finland to define the limits of properties, and they cannot be removed without breaking the law. They are fixed to the ground by three stumps that expand the moment the boxes are pushed into the earth, and there they stay. On older properties the markers may be rocks, trees, or any other object that can be recognized as a fixed point of reference. Sometime a simple red tape ribbon tied to a branch has the same meaning. And nobody removes it.

In 1994 Finland was still recovering from a hard economic depression that had lasted a few years and had hit hard both businesses and private individuals, especially in the country. This was evident and tangible. People's priorities were making ends meet and having food on the table. Designer clothes, cars, and consumable and luxury products were not a priority and were still predominantly strange to the country's forest culture.

The recession had inevitably also hit the housing market and the overall care that people took of their properties. It was reflected in the general status and appearance of the buildings.

Away from the village, houses were still traditionally made of wood, usually boards but occasionally logs that had been painted red or yellow or light grey or pastel blue, with white window frames. Most of them looked tired and a little neglected, in need of new coats of paint, of the odd roof repair, or of a wash. With no exception, they all had small wooden huts of various sizes scattered in the garden and had large stacks of chopped wood almost everywhere, sometimes even just left in the middle of the plots of land. These were neatly piled wood logs, all of the same length (thirty centimetres, we later found out) to fit the baking ovens and the sauna stoves. Two posts at each end of the stack stopped the logs from collapsing, and sometimes a plastic sheet was thrown over to give the wood some cover from rain and—in winter—from snow.

Wood is the all-important fuel in Finnish homes, and a substantial stack of chopped logs gives a wonderful sense of security. It provides the feeling that even when the world is under several feet of snow, or if the Russians may one day decide to cut gas and energy supplies to their small but relentlessly anti-Russian neighbour, the home may still be warm and comfortable, and bread can be baked.

After many years of living in Finland we ourselves know the feeling only too well. At the end of summer, wood is collected or delivered, and one by one the chopped logs are stacked and added to what was left over from the previous winter and from the summer saunas. It looks good to see the piles in the garden from your window, and somehow you feel safe and comfortable.

We tend to get our wood delivered sometime in August. It comes on a large trailer in chopped logs that just need stacking. We try to put as much as possible in the small storage room at the back of the garage in three neat piles about six feet high, and the rest we place in a corner of the garden. The following year the garden stock will be put in the storage room, and the cycle continues. Theoretically, we always try and use the previous year's wood and replace it with the new stock. In practice we never seem to burn enough wood to exhaust the old logs, with the result that the new ones are piled always in front and used before we ever get to the old ones. I am sure that by now the logs stacked at the back of the storage room are probably too old and dry to burn efficiently, even in the sauna stove. Well, at least we feel we always have plenty of wood. It is nice to look at it.

The houses were simple square constructions on a concrete base, often with a tin roof that had gone rusty over the years spent covered in snow. They all appeared to have drain pipes descending from the gutters that ended in just a bend suspended from the ground, to simply let the rain water run onto the grass and soak away into the earth.

They tended to be huddled to one another in small clusters with no borders between gardens, open to onlookers and discretely gossiping neighbours. In some cases the keys were permanently left in the lock, probably forgotten through the knowledge that safety and security are no issues within small communities. We were told that in order to let the neighbours (and everyone else for that matter) know that you are not at home, you just have to put a broom across the door frame. This, we thought, was almost an invitation for potential burglars, and somehow it is a method that we have not come round to trying ourselves yet, our minds corrupted by years of alarm systems, neighbourhood watches, sensor security lights, padlocks, and chains. All we have had the courage to do is leave the windows open and protected only by the mosquito netting when we go out for the day, and even that has taken some serious debating before being put into action. We have become accustomed and have learnt to understand the great feeling of safety and security that this country offers. In a lot of cases, people seem to leave their house keys permanently in the lock outside the door day and night and they sleep in peace. We have done it ourselves, in fact, admittedly by mistake, as we still carry with us our culture of violence and crime. We are learning.

Now we even leave one key in a strategic place outside the house in case we are locked out. We have made some progress. Unfortunately, the only time when the back door slammed shut and locked us outside, the "safety key" was not as yet in its place and we had to rely on a friend, who takes care of our home while we are in England, to come to our rescue with the key we had given him. We felt completely silly.

Safety is one of the major features of this country. It is a safe place. A place where young children can walk alone to school on dark Winter mornings through a wood without danger (that is, of course, apart from possible encounters with wolves, bears, lynx, elks, and so on) and where elderly ladies can live alone in their ancestral homes in the forest, in the knowledge that nothing dreadful might happen to them at the hand of humans.

I vividly recall one winter morning some years ago, when we unusually had to go somewhere at a ridiculously early hour, still in complete darkness. We managed to get in our car at around 8.30, after our two cups each of tea and a coffee with my breakfast of toast and Marmite, and we drove through the sleepy village. Cars are very few and far between at the best of times. At that hour in the middle of winter, the place was deserted. On a corner stood the solitary little figure of a child, wrapped up warm in his winter clothes, carrying a rucksack, his woollen hat down to his eyes. He could not have been older than eight or nine. He was standing still, obviously waiting for a friend to appear and walk with him the rest of the couple of kilometres to school. We looked at him as we drove past, not believing it possible. Then we realized we were in a small village in Finland and felt sure that that child would get to school safe and on time. We never thought of it again. And nothing happened to him, of course.

The gardens were open spaces of land around the houses, where occasionally tentative vegetable plots made their appearance amidst the weeds that had been left to grow to an unreasonable size. The patches of grass were broken by large bunches of low plants that grew everywhere, absorbing every drop of dampness from the ground and developing leaves of immense size. They seemed one of the most common features.

We had some of these invasive and sturdy plants in our garden too, and over the years we have eliminated them, pulling them from the ground with great difficulty. Their long and tuberous roots are solidly embedded into the earth. If left to their own devices, these plants would soon cover vast areas, giving the garden a cumbersome and untidy appearance. Nobody, surprisingly, seemed too bothered with them though, probably because they do not require any attention or care, even in winter. They completely cover the weeds, and they survive with no problem the freezing conditions. I have to say that we hate them and we do not have any left.

Every house had a number of berry bushes next to it, swollen and colourful in their untidy way, sometimes kept upright by plastic "hoola-hoops" around their stems, sometimes covered by mesh to protect their juicy fruits from ever-hungry birds. These bushes are at the same time the pride and the pain of many Finns, for whom berry-picking is a kind of compulsory national occupation. Everyone picks berries, and most people hate doing it. Berries are so important to Finnish country life that a whole chapter will be dedicated to them later.

The drives were not really drives at all. They were generally made out of the two strips that were the result at first of cart wheels and subsequently of car tyres pressing the grass and wearing it out over the years. They just ended into nothing, melting with the rest of the grass.

A lot of the gardens looked a little like dumping grounds, with an array of objects left scattered almost anywhere after use. Snow shovels still leaned against the house walls after winter, and by now probably waiting for next winter. Watering cans, children's toys, plastic sheeting, wood planks, sledges. You could not help feeling that gardens were not important; just a piece of land where anything that did not fit in the house could be left. But of course land is not at a premium here. Land is everywhere. It is empty and is available to everyone. The country's population – half of London's inhabitants – of which at least fifty per cent is concentrated in the southern and western major cities, is scattered over a land larger than Britain. The land is empty, and people can legally go anywhere on the land. Having tools or objects left in your garden is not important. You have the whole of the Finnish forests to yourself.

I remember one day many years ago when we were having an easy lunch with our daughter and (now) her husband on the porch of the log cottage that we had built in an old wood not too far from our village. Suddenly a man appeared through the gates, carrying a plastic bucket. He walked with a purpose on our drive, totally ignoring us, stepped down a small bank, and disappeared into the wood – our wood! I called to him, with the typical English system of saying, "Excuse me … can I help you?" hiding the fact that I was furious at the liberty that this individual was taking. He did not even turn his head, which made me even more furious. I suppose I should have said it in Finnish, but he probably would have laughed at my pronunciation.

I am certain that it was the same gentleman who in the previous Winter, with the ground covered in thick snow, came skiing right through our open gate one day, looked at us and asked for the easiest way down to the lake, and then, with not a word of apology or thanks, disappeared into the wood towards the frozen water edge.

When we told some friends about the mysterious skier, expecting outraged reactions at the man's total disregard for our privacy, we learnt that any piece of land is available to anyone to walk on, pick berries or mushrooms from, ski through, and so on – unless the piece of land is clearly marked as "Private".

The following day, we drove to the nearest town, found a screen-printing company, and had a wonderful yellow and black sign made that read "Private Area", which we fixed to the gate of our log cottage. I wanted to add that "Trespassers Will Be Eaten by Bears", but Celia managed to convince me that the simple description on the sign was sufficient. It seems to have worked, that is at least for everyone except our berry-picking skier with his plastic bucket, who obviously decided to ignore our privacy sign on that summer day. Since then with no exception, all the Finns we have met over the years have been incredibly polite and considerate. I like to think of our "unwanted visitor" as a rare example of ignorance and arrogance. Or – as many Finns might suggest – maybe he was simply Russian!

Some patches of grass appeared to have been mowed, irregularly, as if just to open up spaces at random between the birches, the fir trees and the berry bushes, not so much for aesthetic purposes as for practicality. We could see no garden furniture of any kind, apart from the occasional plastic chair, the very traditional and heavy table and seats made out of half tree trunks, and the complicated frame of swinging wooden benches on a decking that every garden featured with pride.

We ourselves had one of these unusual looking seats at the back of the house. To step on them you risk your life, as the planks making up the decking swing at the same time as the benches. Nothing is stable or fixed, and we have to admire the inventiveness and the design of the contraption that make the whole thing quite comfortable and relaxing once you have managed to get on board, provided you are not trying to recover from a happy night out with friends at a local bar.

We had certainly never seen such swings until we came to Finland. They look complicated and heavy, almost like three-dimensional puzzles. They take up a lot of space in a garden, but they seem to be a must in every Finnish house.

When one of our daughters and her family visited us one summer, they were so enchanted by it that we contacted the maker, through a friend of ours, and had one shipped all the way to Devon for their garden as a surprise present. With typical Finnish efficiency, the swing was delivered quickly to a very remote (and beautiful) hamlet in the middle of the greenest of the English counties.

Back in England during a weekend spent with them, I helped my son-in-law put it up. We had to find our way through the sheet of instructions that luckily were only visual, because otherwise the task of assembling the multitude of pieces of wood together following directions in Finnish would have been too impossible even for an astrophysicist. The complicated structure has now been standing in our daughter's undulating garden for quite some time, and everyone who has seen it or tried the gentle rocking of the swing has been amazed and impressed. It is an amusing little piece of Finland in a Devon country cottage garden.

Over the years we have seen the general conditions in Finland become progressively better, the economy showing growing signs of stability and confidence, and people looking more opulent, albeit in their simple way of life. Houses have become neater, better kept and better painted. Gardens are now beginning to have shapes and purposes that they never had and the grass is even cut regularly and with care.

I remember our first sSummer by the lake. It was August, and we were having some wonderful sunny hot days. Everything was still new to us, and we used to spend a lot of time on the small wobbly jetty, sitting on the wooden boards, enjoying the splashes from the waves when larger boats came past. When we decided that it was time for us to try and sit a little more comfortably on the jetty, we went around looking for garden furniture. All we could find were two small tubular-frame chairs with cloth seats. They were very low on the ground but quite useful. We found them in a long gone hardware store in the next village, after looking in many other shops. I think they came from Brazil of all places. We spent many an hour sunbathing on them.

Now garden furniture of all types and styles is readily available almost anywhere, and the proliferation of gardening magazines and TV programs has created an explosion of interest in all things related to gardens, be it tools, parasols, shades, or watering accessories. A number of large and well-laid garden centres have appeared in different locations, which have little to envy to their older and more established counterparts in England. Only some of the plants familiar to us in England are missing, simply because they would just not survive winters in the Finnish freezer.

All large stores now carry a vast range of gardening tools with famous international brands – shears, secateurs, hoes, extendable choppers, strimmers, and so on. Everything is available, with the exception of one particular object that to this day we have not seen anywhere in Finland – the vertical blade trimmer, so useful for tidying edges of grass and circles around trees. This simply does not exist in Finland and it is because there are as yet no edges to trim. The gardens are simply left to mix with drives and paths and tree bases left to the aggression of growing grass.

Some years ago we decided to give one of these long-handled vertical shears to a good friend whose interest, love, and ability for gardening has slowly transformed her farmhouse land in the middle of a forest into a delightful and colourful garden. We bought two of these tools in a garden centre in England, packed them in bubble wrap and cardboard and put them through the "exceptional luggage" x-ray machine at Heathrow. We picked them up at Vantaa airport and gave one to our friend as a Christmas present, knowing full well that it could not be used for at least another six months. I think she has mastered its use and some of her flower and vegetable beds now have a resemblance of a clear edge around them, after a lot of hard digging work – when the snow is not covering them of course. So there are now two such sets of shears in Finland.

I still remember the first time we saw a local handyman cut the grass in the rough field around a bar/coffee place by the village harbour. We were having a relaxing drink on the terrace overlooking the lake, admiring the different boats moored by the jetties stretching far into the water. He was using a hand-pushed lawnmower that looked at least thirty years old and a bit sorry for itself, with no rear bag for the collection of the cuttings. He was walking in a line, pushing the machine with an expression that said he clearly would rather be at home watching TV, or out with his friends enjoying a glass or more of Vina. Once at the end of the run, instead of simply steering the machine round and go forward again, he would pull the lawnmower all the way back and start pushing it to cut another stretch of grass, covering the same distance twice, taking twice the time and leaving the whole place suffocated in grass cuttings. He was not the exception. We saw the same exercise time and again on several different occasions, and we did not quite understand the sense of it. At the time it simply seemed to be the Finnish way of cutting the grass – just a little amusing.

Things have changed now. The technique – or the lack of it – has become more accurate and practical, although it has lost some of its amusing aspects. The whole world is becoming boringly too equal.

As to our garden, Juhani kindly offered to let me use his sit-on mower to keep the grass under control. I had never used one before, and after a learning period, I enjoyed driving the machine around the trees and the rocks, although it proved totally inadequate because of the nature of the garden, which had been created out of a field and still had dips and bumps and rocks. Its surface was irregular and uneven and there were a lot of trees. The mower also had the rotating blade right under the seat in the very centre, and this made it virtually impossible to mow the grass up to the edges of the garden. I began to understand why only a minute patch of grass had ever been mowed, around the house and in the centre, away from trees, rocks and plant beds. That was the easy way. It was also a rather old machine, and every now and then the rubber belt controlling the blade would give up the ghost and the whole thing would stop. The problem must have been occurring for some considerable time, because Juhani, with his mechanical inventiveness, had even replaced a piece of the belt with a metal chain, but the illness had not been cured. So every fifteen minutes on average, I had to tilt the machine and fiddle about with the belt and the chain until they had the necessary tension and start it again. Not really ideal.

I am no gardener by any means, but I have a pretty good idea on how to keep a garden tidy. So I started cutting by hand the tall grass and the weeds that had invaded everywhere, and I slowly began to discover the boundaries of the plot of land. What we thought was still garden turned out to be lake and where we thought was water turned out to be land. Many trees became visible and one tall standing light came to life, looking surprised to find out that its purpose was again to illuminate the garden and not to hide its face behind bushes. It was all laborious and time consuming.

After some relatively encouraging success, we finally decided that some help was needed. Apart from the difficulty of penetrating a long neglected "jungle" with hand tools, the time required to improving the garden, added to our long absences during the weeks that we would spend back in England, called for someone to be found who could take care of most of the mowing and the weeding.

It is amazing how fast things grow in Finland. Nature seems to be moving at a unique speed. Everything is covered by snow and ice for almost six months during the year, and the seeds planted in autumn do not start showing any sign of growth until May. Then suddenly by late June, crops seem to have caught up with their cousins from warmer climates, taking all of two months to achieve what normally takes at least double that time. The long hours of light in the summer months push nature to accelerate its step, and you can almost watch the explosion of the fresh shoots happen in front of your eyes, almost as soon as the snow and the ice disappear from the ground.

The trouble is, of course, that weeds and grass also grow at the same speed, which means that, left on their own without any disciplinary action; they invade every corner of a garden as soon as you give them some rest from weed-killers and cutters. Being absent for a month and leaving the garden to its own temperament during the Spring and Summer months means returning to a forest and to an even greater invasion of mosquitos. It was therefore essential that we should find someone prepared to spend some time looking after our patch in the way we liked, without considering us ridiculously pedantic.

Once we got to know a few people, we had a very interesting and effective hint from a local land owner who has a substantial business in farming his many hectares of land. The best and fastest cure against weeds is pickling vinegar. Trusting his advice, we went on an expedition to the local supermarket to buy the vinegar. We found it in large plastic bottles and in very large plastic tubs. We bought a number of each. Back home we mixed the vinegar with water in a watering can, careful to keep to the portions that had been suggested to us – two parts of water and one of vinegar, and I walked along the drive spraying the contents. When I had finished, the drive smelled like a nicely mixed salad, but the following day the weeds were dry and dead!

We have been using the procedure ever since, and we do feel that the local supermarkets must have been wondering why suddenly over the last five or six years there has been a surge in pickling activity among the village housewives. No sooner does the stock of pickling vinegar come on the shelves than the stock disappears. Maybe some local people have had to go without their pickled gherkins or onions for some time now, but at least our drive is clear of weeds.

Back to our search for a gardener. It was easier said than done. It proved very difficult to find anyone. Gardening was not part of the local culture. Weeding was a job for ladies who looked after their flower beds. Gardeners and garden designs did not exist. Additionally, the general "that will do" philosophy of the Finns is such that details are often neglected. This is reflected in all aspects of everyday life. The extra push to be given to a door that does not shut properly, the corner of a step that is not perfectly aligned to the others, the floor boards that creek or have gaps in between; all this is undoubtedly less important than life itself or the forests. We know that perfection does not exist and instead of becoming stressed by this realization, the Finns sensibly accept it, relax and get on with doing what they enjoy doing. So weeds or uneven paths or long grass by trees in a garden are not that important. Let's put them into perspective and at the end of the list. The Finns may be right, and no doubt over the years we have ourselves become lazier and more tolerant about imperfections, but we still wanted our garden to look nice. Maybe it is an English obsession.

The village had a small number of well-known handymen who were well equipped with machinery of all kinds and who were capable of solving any problem that involved heavy work, digging, lifting, earth moving and the like. They could certainly cut our grass and remove rocks or chop trees, but gardening as a job that requires an attention to details was alien to them. Also, inevitably, we were not yet "locals", and we were rather low in their scale of priorities. Very often some kind of emergency seemed to suddenly occur somewhere else, and they simply did not turn up at all. It was a bit frustrating, but it appeared common practice, and we had no intention of trying to change old habits after only weeks in our village. The result was that we had to resort to buying a lawnmower of our own, and frequently I had to do the job myself. The part I hated most was empting the bag full with the grass cuttings. Many a time I was tempted to leave the bag off the mower and let the grass spread freely over the garden, the same as I had seen the gentleman do by the harbour coffee place, but then I remembered our comments and I felt bad. So the grass cuttings were emptied, with a grunt.

Paula – our friend who with Tuomo took us to the midnight picnic in the forest in mid-Winter – helped us find a student willing to take up the task as a summer job. Paula was at the time working for the 4H organization, a well-known institution that trains young and old to care for the land and the forests, and she knew of many students who were interested in forestry and agriculture. So she introduced us to a nice young girl by the name of Henna who one summer spent an immense number of hours doing almost nothing to the garden, apart from showing good will at a slow pace. She was no gardener but a very pleasant teenager, who at least kept the weeds at bay during the times we spent back in England. We have lost trace of Henna, who no doubt found a more interesting job after completing her university studies. We wish her well.

For the last few years a couple of young lads from the local school have been looking after the garden and the house. Another friend of ours suggested at first the son of some people he knew well. Ari was his name and he came to see us as a shy teenager, hesitant to use his limited English and very pleased to be able to make some money to help his motocross passion. He needed some training and had to get used to what must have looked to him as the rather peculiar and boring ways of an elderly English couple.

He was very young and had to get accustomed to his first " boss " and to a different way of thinking that was a far cry from the Finnish approach to relations, where often things are not told face to face but through third parties so as not to upset people. (Generally, the result is that people get upset anyway.)

Ari discovered that straight talking does not necessarily mean arguments or break-ups and that I never keep grudges. I remember one day when Ari did not appear at the usual time. After waiting some half an hour, I decided that the delay was totally unacceptable in view of the religious punctuality of the Finns, and I called him on his mobile phone. His excuse was that he had to go somewhere. I severely told him off for not letting me know in advance and made it clear that I was not to be ignored. Ari came to see me later and was clearly shaken and worried, justifying his rather superficial approach with the fact that he had other things to do as well as looking after our garden. I explained that I was prepared to accept anything except unreliability or lack of communication, and I certainly could never accept being treated with contempt or neglect. As far as I was concerned, that was the end of the discussion. No more was said and no grudges were held. Ari has become a young friend of ours with a lot of respect and possibly admiration. He has understood that saying things face to face does not mean that people have to become enemies.

Over the years he learnt to maintain the garden in an impeccable way, to the amazement of everyone who has seen our place. He ended his school and unfortunately went into the army, a grown young man, but before he went he made sure that he would find a friend who could continue in his footsteps. And he did. We often see him and his pretty girlfriends who from time to time have appeared in his life. Time seems to have passed very quickly.

Tomi came onto the scene; another teenager from the same school, who proved to be as capable and as reliable as Ari, so the garden continued looking splendid, and we could leave the place in the relaxing knowledge that on our return it will be exactly as we wish it to be. We have been fortunate.

Nowadays most gardens around the village are cared for with an attention and a passion that certainly did not exist when we first came to Finland. Motor mowers are everywhere and people have mastered the art of cutting the grass in stripes and clearing the tree bases from weeds. It is a reflection of the better living standards and maybe of the little part we may have played in awakening the desire to enjoy tidy gardens to the full in the short span of time between two winters. As I said earlier, the world is becoming too equal.

We had never been inside a Finnish home lived by Finns, and the first time we did so was on Christmas Eve. We met Juhani and his family around midnight (we were beginning to think that everything in Finland happened at night.) We met in the local cemetery – as you do of course - where they had lit candles for their dead relatives, as most people in the village did, before going back home to a warming fire and to the Christmas food. We were asked back to the apartment that Juhani had bought after moving out of his house for us and while waiting to move to Spain.

The place was extremely tidy, immaculately clean, and very warm, especially after walking the short distance from the cemetery in temperatures of 30 degrees below zero. We took our shoes off, as everyone does when entering a home. You rarely walk into someone's home with your shoes on; it is impolite and messy, especially in winter, when blobs of snow would drop to the floor and leave marks on the wooden boards. Shoes are always left in the entrance, sometimes tidily hidden in a cupboard, but generally left on the floor, giving the entrance the look of a place hit by a storm or even an earthquake. You walk around in socks – or barefooted in the summer – and if pets live in the home as well, you carry back to your own place the usual amount of hair. But, I suspect that Finnish pets are tutored well enough to learn that they have to drop their hair only in allowed places and – being Finnish – they are very observant of all laws and regulations.

We have long adopted the system of taking spare house shoes with us when visiting friends. An easy way to be polite and at the same time feel the comfort and safety of shoes on our feet; it is a system that some of our friends have now taken up themselves. It eliminates embarrassing situations, like the time when we were invited to dinner by some very nice people in their Tampere apartment. The very same people who have transformed their old family farmhouse in the forest, not too far from our village, into a wonderful showpiece of Finnish traditional home environment, surrounded by a delightful and natural garden.

It was winter and we decided that it would be wise to spend the night in a Tampere hotel, so as not to have to rush back, driving some ninety kilometres on an infamous icy road, without even enjoying a glass of wine with our friends. Finland has very strict laws when it comes to drinking and driving. I enjoy a drink or two myself, but as a matter of principle, wherever I am, I never drink a drop of alcohol when I know I am going to drive.

I remember the time on one particular May 1st (one of the many major days of celebrations for the Finns, when drinks are consumed in very large quantities) when we were asked to dinner by the same friends, this time at their forest abode, which features a great gazebo in the garden. The journey involved a drive of eleven kilometres of deserted forest road, with only scattered log houses making their appearance amidst trees.

At the turning point, where the road reaches the corner of a stunningly beautiful lake and becomes a dirt tack, we were stopped by two Police patrol cars on a random check of drivers. My polite salutations in Finnish were answered by one of the officers, who in perfect English explained that I had to take a little "alcohol test" and produced the small device with a short plastic tube for me to blow hard into. This was the first time ever for me. The test was negative – as was to be expected – and the officer, in English, wished us a good journey. Our car was the only one on the road and maybe the only one that had gone by in several hours. This was scary, and it was certainly the proof that it is not worth drinking at the risk of a substantial fine and the embarrassment, even in the middle of a forest.

So – back to our winter stay in Tampere - we packed the essentials for a night away, and much to my horror once in the hotel, I discovered that I had a hole in the heel of one of my thermal woollen socks and I had not brought with me an extra pair. I sat all evening trying to hide my feet, crossing them under the chair, conscious of the hole that, in my mind, was attracting everyone's attention. It was terrible.

Since that first time we have seen many Finnish homes. They mostly have wooden floor boards, very often painted in beautiful pastel colours that would never be conceivable in England, where the light is different, and less crisp, and where the houses are mostly of bricks and cement, carpets cover the floors from wall to wall, and wallpaper covers the walls. There are always plenty of colourful rugs, generally made by local cottage industries. Occasionally they have a cellar to accommodate the water pump and to store some of the many bottles of berry juices that are prepared in autumn.

Impressed with the colours and the quality of most of the rugs, we bought some from the local makers with the view to take them back to our home in England, as a reminder of Finland. The shopkeepers made up very neat parcels for us to carry on our flights as hand luggage. The material and the colours were extremely good, with contrasting tones of blue, green, yellow, and even brown, all nicely melting in tasteful combinations, so suitable for the wooden floors and for both the crisp light of Finnish Summers and the soft tones of candles and fire flames in winter.

They just did not suit England, where the air is heavier with pollution; the layout of the gardens, the lighting, the fireplaces; – the rugs simply looked wrong. It was a good example of how impossible is to reproduce an environment in the absence of all the ingredients.

And the same applies in the opposite direction.

Years later when we finally purchased the log house from Juhani, we had some furniture shipped from England, including a beautiful oak folding leaf dinner table, rather antique, that we felt would be perfect for a particular corner of the sitting room. When it arrived and was unpacked, it just looked terribly out of place. Maybe it was its dark oak colour; maybe it was because of the bare log walls or the varnished floor boards or the large windows that let so much light in; or maybe just the complicated structure of the legs. Whatever the reason, a piece that had looked wonderful in our Edwardian home in England looked awful in Finland. Much to our consternation and disappointment, the table is now in the sitting room of the summer sauna, standing in a corner, covered by a cloth. Very sad.

The sitting rooms or the lounges are the most important spaces in the Finnish house – after the sauna, of course. That is where the large fireplaces are the dominant feature. These used to be of old granite stone or ceramic; now they are often in soapstone, a kind of smooth granite-like material that has the ability to store heat for some considerable time and warm the whole house.

Traditionally, old farmhouses were long buildings in timber on one floor, with interconnected rooms, so as to maximise the light in winter. They often had a very large common room (the tupa), in which the farm labourers used to congregate after a hard day's work, sitting on the long wooden benches by the walls, looking at the huge fire place and chatting about country matters, the weather temperament and hunting, while women kept themselves busy baking or knitting.

The friends we visited in their Tampere apartment have such a farmhouse, close to a splendid lake surrounded by beautiful and thick forests. The old character has been religiously maintained, along with the typical features of the old tupa. Many a time we have sat on the worn-out bench that runs along two of the long walls of the huge room. The wood has almost been polished by the numerous behinds that have perched on it over its many years of existence. The edges are smooth and rounded, making almost a wooden cushion out of the thick plank. The imposing whitewashed fireplace takes up a third of the room and now offers a warm sleeping place to the well-trained cats, after giving comfort and security to the labourers in years gone by. The long poles on which the rings of rye bread used to be dried are still there, by the ceiling, reminders of long dark evenings spent by the farm labourers chatting about the daily events and of their ladies talking about making bread and jam. The place has a unique atmosphere of isolation, tradition, pride and nature.

The rooms that seem to have the least importance in the Finn's home culture have always been the bedrooms and the bathrooms. These are just accessories, places where you sleep and clean yourself, without the need for any special comfort, and places that ought to take up as little room as possible within the home.

The bedrooms are, well, just bedrooms. One bed - double or single - generally takes up a corner that seems unimportant and is not used for anything else. The bed or beds are squeezed in, often against the wall on one side. You have to scramble into bed at night, feeling agile and young – or tired and old – climbing over someone else's legs and feet in order to reach your place. Or you can simply not go to bed.

I remember a place we visited years later, when it looked as if Juhani wanted to get back to his house. His Spanish adventure in Fuengirola having turned into a miserable failure, because the expected pleasures of life in the sun had resulted in him living in a densely populated area full of Finnish expatriates.

We had started looking around for alternative accommodations that would enable us to stay in Finland and allow us to continue to enjoy the clean air and the beauty of the country. We were driven round by a kind of estate Agent from the village, who took it upon himself to show us something that we might like, after being spoiled by our existing, very comfortable accommodation.

We happened one day to drive to a place by a lake (what else?) owned by a middle-aged couple who showed us round, describing everything in impeccable English. The house was not large, but it was very well kept. There were a number of outbuildings that culminated in the most unbelievable garage. It had every imaginable tool hanging on the walls, as well as a collapsible table purposely fitted for gutting animals, especially elks, after a day of culling. It was a sort of rustic operating table for animal victims.

The drive, gently sloping down to the lake, was immaculately clean and even enjoyed underground heating in order to make it easier to drive on in winter. The house had a large sauna, with its own balcony overlooking the lake, for relaxation,

The one thing that was obviously missing was the toilet. An electric loo had been installed in the garage, but we were told that this could not operate in winter anyway.

When we asked the lady of the house how they would cope with calls of nature, she candidly replied, "Well, we do cope. We are Finnish." Did she mean that they could cope because they could willingly develop acute cases of constipation that lasted a year or so, or did she mean that Finnish people can survive without a bathroom and can be proud of it? Whatever the answer, the conclusion is that this nice middle-aged Finnish couple, well-educated and polite, did not regard the toilet or the bathroom in general as an essential item within the house.

We found this amazing.

I cannot as yet stop feeling that in this acceptance of hardship – almost a deliberate choice – in the twenty-first century and in a country which has become one of the most technologically advanced in the world; there must be a strong element of self-glorification and theatrical exhibitionism. Finns love to depict themselves to the world at large as constant victims of dreadful weather extremes and of an impossibly hard and troubled past. Somehow they feel that in this way they can acquire the identity of a nation which is unique and capable of coping with the struggles of life and which is different from all others. It is probably a way to find a unity and a national spirit that has come so late for Finland.

It may be that the couple genuinely followed this pattern and made a point of underlining the ever-present belief: the Finnish poor and difficult past and its consequent discomfort are all intrinsic elements of this proud country, a country that still today is desperately trying to find its own place on the world stage, without realizing that in fact its industrial achievements and its international image have already placed it among the best.

But I am digressing. To return to the topic of Finnish homes, bathrooms did not exist. Only recently have interior magazines started to feature bathrooms as spaces to be thought of within the general content of a home. There are still small shower rooms – or cubicles – where the shower is simply a jet that covers the floor with an immense quantity of water. In these rooms there are no shower curtains and no shower walls. (I believe this is amusingly - and with no great imagination - called in English a "wet room". Yes it does get wet!). You have a shower and the walls; the door, the toilet seat, the basin, and you just get wet, very wet. The gentle gradient towards the plug-hole in the middle of the tiled floor only allows the water to run away slowly and in small doses. The best way to avoid any rising damp and to walk out of the cubicle without leaving a line of wet footprints everywhere is mopping. It is so nice at the end of a working day being able to have a relaxing hot shower and then having to mop the floor before you dry yourself!

In essence, bathrooms are just not perceived as rooms that need particularly appetising furniture and comfort. But, on the other hand, the saunas and the lake offer wonderful alternatives.

Back to the nice couple whose house did not have a toilet. Their bedroom was on the first floor of the log house, a kind of mezzanine floor between the ground and the high point of the angled roof, in what would be considered a loft under the elevations. Because of the roof gradient you could in fact stand erect only in its middle. Moving away from the very centre meant having to progressively bend and then kneel and then crawl. The room was spacious and comfortable. The only trouble was getting there. A steep set of wooden steps was leaning against the railing of the loft, standing in the middle of the open plan lounge. Going to bed meant climbing up the precarious steps. Quite frankly, after a night with friends and a few drinks sprawled in the comfortable armchairs of the sitting room below, I could not imagine anything more dangerous than going to sleep in that house.

I had visions of us, once upstairs, remembering that the light in the sauna had not been switched off or that the meat that Celia had left out in the kitchen to defrost for the following evening's dinner had not been put into the fridge. Just the thought of having to use those impossible steps again would have meant higher electricity bills and a number of wasted meals.

On the other hand, this same house had a very comfortable and spacious sauna, with a smaller room leading to it, where it was possible to sit and relax in between perspiration sessions and enjoy a beer or two. The design of the house was just based on different priorities from what we had been used to.

As to the sauna, this is in fact probably the most important room of a Finnish home, and it certainly deserves its own separate chapter.

All windows in Finnish houses have triple glazing, something that was new to us. In fact our hundred-year-old Edwardian house in England has only single glazing and a lot of gaps around the window frames. It is not the warmest of the places even in the comparatively warm English Winters, despite a good central-heating system. Mind you, single-pane windows are easier to clean – a meagre consolation. In Finland one summer's day we decided to clean our triple-glazed windows. It was an operation that required particular skills. Once the windows were open, the two internal frames could be set apart and we were confronted by three sets of glass panes to clean. We completed the job, managing to fix the two internal frames again and then close the whole window.

The following winter, as soon as the temperature dropped to minus 20 degrees, the windows – especially in the kitchen where their size is immense – froze in between the frames. It became impossible to see through them, and everything in the garden and on the frozen lake was but a blur. The minute amount of dampness that had remained between the frames after we had cleaned the glass in the summer had now frozen. We have learnt since then that the space in between the frames must be left to dry completely before fixing the three layers of the windows again. Winters in Finland are special. It is a problem that our draughty English windows will never have.

Over the years we have seen a dramatic transformation in the Finns' perception of the home, its design, and its furnishing. Magazines of all descriptions and tastes are now readily available even from supermarket shelves, showing so much interior design and furnishing that people are not only spoilt for choice but are even confused. Names and concepts that had been familiar only to a privileged few are now commonly accepted and recognised. Once again the world is sadly becoming more and more equal, and individual characteristics are disappearing under the unstoppable steamroller of global marketing.

Hopefully, the Finnish forests will continue to be the healthy and sensible factors that influence Finnish lives. There are no Prada trees or Gucci rocks there; just healthy, old-fashioned, steady nature.

The Sauna

Someone once told me that as soon as they arrived in the African desert to fight with the Allies in World War II, the Finnish troops set up a tent in the middle of their camp and made a sauna out of it. It would appear inconceivable that in the scorching temperatures of the African sun and on the burning sand of the desert, a sauna could even be thought of.

The thing is that for the Finns, the sauna is not just a hot room; it is a way of thinking, almost a religion, something that over the years we ourselves have learnt to understand and appreciate. Saunas are not an enjoyment. They are a need and a tradition, a way for the Finns to ensure and maintain their roots close to nature.

As much as in England people would not even think of asking whether a new house or apartment has bathroom and toilet facilities, so in Finland people cannot even imagine the possibility of a house or an apartment without the sauna. It has always been so, since the few scattered tribal communities started living in the thick forests.

Saunas are now common in most countries. Health centres, sport establishments, swimming pools, gyms, hotels, all feature sauna rooms in white tiles, with elaborate benches, designer lights, electric heaters. They are often confused with Turkish baths and steam rooms. People sit in the heat for ten minutes without even a drop of water being thrown on the hot stones, and then go and relax on comfortable loungers in cooler rooms with tiled walls and fancy lighting, feeling fashionable, modern and generally exhausted. It is another example of a pastime that has been forcibly introduced into societies obsessed with imitation, status symbols, hurry, and general disinterest.

Traditionally, Finnish saunas have been tiny wooden huts, somewhere in the garden or in the wood, not too close to the house and, if possible, close to a water edge. Small constructions with a small window, a stove (kivas), and a couple of wooden benches at different levels. Apparently, the correct way to build a sauna is in fact to have one bench at the same height as the top of the stove so that the feet are at level with the hot stones and another bench about fifty centimetres higher than the first to sit upon. I was told that in this way the blood circulation is maximised and the body receives the most amount of heat from the stove. I have of course no way – nor the inclination - to prove or disprove this theory. All saunas I have seen are built to follow this concept. It must be the right way.

Driving through the Finnish countryside it is common to spot minute huts almost hidden among the trees, sometimes leaning a little due to their age and the subsidence of the ground that has been softened and hardened by millennia of different temperatures. You recognise these huts as old saunas because of the small chimneys shooting out of the tin roofs. Generations after generations have spent time in there, sweating out the day's labour and the dust from the corn fields. Now they just barely stand, tiny monuments of traditions; occasionally still used for their original purpose; more often than not neglected and forgotten. Their place has been taken over by more modern saunas in the houses – electric, fast and boring. Even here people are beginning to succumb to the desire for speed and comfort. It is regrettable and sad, but inevitable.

Often saunas have a small deck or balcony where one can sit and get refreshed with a cool drink in between sessions by the stove. They have always been places for relaxation, cleansing, talking, and thinking. You do not hurry in the sauna, if it is a real sauna.

Dim light is provided by the tiny window, during spring and summer days or by the gentle indoor light, traditionally toned down and filtered through a wooden box-like cover with a series of wooden angled flaps. This gives a mystic character to the room, as do the aroma of the burning wood, the splashing of the water on the hot stones, the tingly feeling from the hot air boosted by the fast vanishing steam and occasionally the added perfume of the koivu essence mixed in the water. Koivu is the silver beech, the most popular of Finnish trees, along with the pine. The essence extracted from the koivu, as well as from the eucalyptus or other aromatic trees, is added to the water and gives a strange sense of purification and mystery when the water is thrown on the hot granite stones. Saunas are for meditation, conversation, decisions and, of course, perspiration. In the sauna everyone is bare, equal, classless.

Many fundamental decisions have been taken in saunas, be they political, business, or family decisions. People invite friends to have saunas over a whole evening with sausages and beer, in the same way as we would normally invite friends for dinner. We have done it ourselves. Celia would be chatting with her friend in the sitting room over a gin and tonic or a glass of juice, while her friend's husband and I would be sitting in the sauna, exchanging opinions on the world at large, talking about our work and perspiring, while nice fat sausages cooked in the pan suspended on a chain over the stove.

And after the pores have been opened by temperatures averaging eighty degrees (many people like to boost their ability to bear much higher temperatures, but I personally feel that eighty is a very respectable one Any higher, and you enter the realm of masochism.) a cool shower or a dip in the nearby lake are at the same time refreshing, cleansing and pleasant.

I honestly enjoy saunas. I enjoy them in the Summer, when nothing is better than a gentle swim in the cool lake to balance the heat after a session by the stove, and in Winter, when many a time I have rolled my body, hot and wet with perspiration, in deep snow at temperatures of minus twenty-five or thirty, proving to myself that I can still do crazy things at my age and that I still possess an inner death wish. The official justification that I give myself and others for this insane pastime is the pleasure of the tingly sensation of the blood as it rushes through the body at the sharp contrast of temperatures. The unspoken truth is probably more a theatrical wish to prove something of no importance, like the ability to enjoy extremes and the self-pleasing fantasy of remaining young and strong. Whatever the reason, the sense of well-being after a sauna and a dive in the snow is no doubt real and good.

I remember with pleasure one New Year's Eve, when Markku and Arja invited us to spend the last hours of 2002 over a plate of crayfish, gloriously refreshed by frozen vodka. Markku and I would have a sauna prior to dinner.

When we arrived at their place by the lake at around 6.00 in the evening, it was pitch dark. We could not even see the lake edge, at the end of the garden. The snow was deep, but the house was warm and welcoming, still glowing with the lights of the Christmas that had just gone. After a preliminary drink Markku and I went into the sauna in one of the old outbuildings. The small balcony outside the sauna room was lit up by candles, and a few bottles of beer had been laid out for the occasional rest in between the hot sessions. We sat in the steamy darkened room, talking of business, of future plans and of family matters.

We took a couple of short breaks for a drink, sitting outside by the snow, giving our bodies just enough time to cool down before returning to the sauna. Some two hours and a few beers later, we re-joined the ladies for a glass of champagne and sat down to dinner, until the time came to welcome in the New Year. It was all very civilized. I felt clean, lightheaded, and fulfilled. Life, after all, is made up of simple pleasures and the Finnish sauna is certainly one of them.

Even our grandsons have experienced the sauna and they love it. Despite their young age, they seem to have captured the purpose and the spirit of the Finnish sauna. They have spent time with me and their father chatting about various things, perspiring, enjoying the sudden surge of temperature when they use the long-handled ladle to throw water on the hot stove, having a welcome cool drink of juice during the short breaks, and finally jumping in the lake for a swim before eating the plump hot sausages that have been cooking over the stove.

Nowadays saunas can be electric, especially in apartments. They are cleaner, faster, and generally more practical. They can be left switched on all the time and as soon as some water is poured over them, the temperature reaches the desired level. I still prefer the old wood-burning saunas and the ritual they demand: getting the logs, filling the stove, lighting the fire, getting the water ready in the wooden bucket, adding the koivu essence to the water, going back to the sauna time and again to check that the wood is burning properly and that the temperature is growing nicely. A sauna is not simply the act of sitting on a wooden bench covered in perspiration. It is a complete ceremony that for a while detaches you from the daily chores. Reducing the sauna to the mere technicality of an electric switch is like making an artist paint with a brush but no colours.

I am told that the ultimate in sauna pleasure is a savu (smoke) sauna, followed by a jump into an opening made in the frozen lake. One day I may try the first, as I am intrigued by what has been described to me as a "black" sauna, where thick smoke has previously covered everything in soot. However, I am not really sure about the latter. The thought of disappearing naked under the ice and never being found again gives me some considerable doubt, not to mention the shock to my tired and ageing limbs and the danger of a starving Mr Pike taking a bite at some precious – and by then frozen – parts. As they say in Finland, ehka, maybe. All I have managed so far has been to break the ice on the lake near the shore, where the depth is about sixty centimetres, and sit in the water after a sauna. Once, when the ice was quickly covering the surface again, I thought of breaking it with my bare feet before dipping in the water. When I went back for a welcome drink, Celia noticed that my feet were bleeding. The ice had cut them like sharp glass, and in the icy water I had not noticed it.

Even saunas can be dangerous.

We had the proof of that once, when we saw a very strange contraption pass in front of our kitchen window, gently floating and moving with the ripple of the lake. It was a small log house with a window and a metal chimney; it had a narrow passageway with a low railing around it. It was a floating sauna with a small boat engine. Some local people had decided that it would be fun to have saunas while enjoying the pleasures of the lake, maybe some fishing in between the hot sessions, diving into Paijanne to cool down. Excellent idea!

Unfortunately, one day while the sauna enthusiasts were enjoying their perspiration and their beer, the mobile sauna decided to go its own way in the hands of Paijanne's currents and ended quite close to a small cruiser aiming for the village harbour. There was no contact, but the wake from the cruiser made the sauna rock enough for the hot stones to fall off the stove and for the whole floating sauna to capsize, severely burning the naked occupants. They had to be rescued and taken to the local hospital for treatment.

We have seen the floating sauna pass by our window since this burning episode. I believe that the owners may have improved its balance and probably installed safety belts too. Finns are crazy about their saunas.

The Village

Once unpacked and settled in our Finnish home, the first thing we had to do was go to the village for the usual food and groceries shopping. The fridge was empty and the freezer emptier. We also wanted to see what the village was like. We had only managed a little glimpse of it when we had come to see the house and met Juhani a couple of months earlier. It was just a name on the map, cut in half by what seemed a curving tape connecting Helsinki to the far north.

One main road. Two supermarkets, four banks, a post office, a flower shop, a Town Hall, a set of shops selling films, herbal remedies, material, watches, jewellery and electrical goods. Nothing else. We saw the famous – or perhaps wrongly infamous – Tehi Bar, where regulars and innocuous addicted drinkers sat on stools peering out of the windows from opening to closing time. The imposing Church with its sharp steeple and wooden-tiled roof in need of a new coat of terva, the tar-based gluey material that gives wooden roofs a brilliantly clean look and a perfect water sealing. A coffee place with petrol pumps. All in all, not much. Oh, sorry, there was a very nice chemist. The large portion of elderly people out of the 3,000 souls living in the village area made it an absolute necessity for the village to have a chemist. The two ladies behind the counter, in their immaculately white overalls, never really tried their best to smile and make customers feel a bit better. I am glad to say that the chemist shop is still in its place and the people now running it are extremely pleasant – and they also speak perfect English. I feel terribly colonial in saying it, but it is a help!

Being July, - holiday time -the village was busy and all of the twenty or so spaces in the one and only car park, opposite one of the supermarkets, were taken by locals and summer visitors. There seemed to be a buzzing feeling all around.

One particular car caught our attention. It had a British registration plate. We were most intrigued to find a compatriot in such a small village in the very middle of Finland and when the driver came out of a shop and walked towards his car, I approached him and asked him where he was from, something I would never dream of doing back home. British culture does not allow for such errors of etiquette Back at home you would never openly go up to strangers and ask them up front where they come from. It has to be done subtly, starting with the weather and its temperament, going on to menial topics like their car or so and finally coming to the main question. This question is always put to them quickly while looking away, almost in a whisper. "Have you come from far?" hoping that the answer will satisfy your curiosity.

But we were in a small Finnish village, and someone had suddenly appeared from nowhere who might spoil our happiness at finding a peaceful oasis away from the world and who might suddenly want a share of the beauty that we felt was only ours.

He turned out to be a local gentleman who in fact lived near London and who was back in the village for the summer. He seemed pleasant enough and we almost forgave him for driving a Jaguar with the familiar number plates. He also inquired (in perfect English) about our reason for being in Finland. He apparently had heard of an English family choosing his village as an escape heaven and he was bemused. By the end of our short conversation, we knew that his son lived only a few hundred meters from us in England and that he himself knew our house, having passed it many times on the way to his son's. Finland is a very large and empty country and Britain has over sixty million inhabitants. Is the world getting too small?

Years later in England, I was in the local surgery having a chat with our doctor after a brief consultation. Inevitably, I was talking about Finland and our love for the country. He mentioned that he had some Finnish patients who had established themselves in our small town. Yes, you are ahead of me. The patients were the family of the gentleman who drove a British-registered Jaguar through our Finnish village. The doctor and I had a good laugh at life's jokes.

We decided that for reasons of practicality we ought to have a bank account with a local bank. After all, it was our intention to come regularly to Finland for the next few years. Somehow we wanted to feel established and have a foothold in the system. So we walked into Postipankki, the Post Office Bank. No explanation for this particular choice. Postipankki was just a name to us. It just happened to be on our side of the main road that cut the village in two. Mind you, it was not that the intensity of the traffic would have made it difficult to cross over and go to Merita (as the now Nordea Bank was called at the time). Cars were few and far between. We simply took the easiest and laziest option.

After an insignificant number of formalities and having been required to provide a surprisingly few pieces of information, we walked out of Postipankki into the July sunshine with a few hundred Markka in our Finnish account. It could not have taken us longer than fifteen minutes and I cannot honestly remember whether we even had to show our passports. So, quickly and with no problems, we had our Finnish bank account.

The Post Office has now long gone, together with Postipankki (which has been taken over by a major insurance company). It is the result of the usual trend in most countries, where local post offices are eliminated in the name of efficiency and economic targets. (How I detest that phrase!) I have to say that the two ladies behind the counter, who dealt with parcels and letters and stamps and bank accounts and money, never looked happy in their job. I think, in fact, that they always tried to do their best to make you feel embarrassed to take money out of your account.

Those times have unfortunately disappeared and been forgotten. I am sure that today, even in this trusting country, the Bin Laden effect has resulted in a much more stringent examination of credentials before a bank account may be opened and in a much deeper scrutiny of transactions. In England we are used to being regularly asked for our granny's pet's name together with our parents' preferred music, the neighbour's underwear colour and the laundry receipts before anything can be done with a bank or a credit card company. Maybe that Finland, with its small population, has not arrived at such extremes yet, but I feel sure that even here it would now take us longer than fifteen minutes to open a new account. The problem here, though, might be that in our village people do not seem to use laundry services, and it would be near to impossible for us to produce the name of our grannies' pets, as they never had any.

When a couple of years later we heard through the proverbial grapevine that Postipankki would close the village branch, we decided to finally cross the road and move our account to Merita. Once again we were impressed by the smooth and simple formalities involved.

The Post Office disappeared, with no traumas or tribulations for the villagers, and the services were taken over by one of the supermarkets. A corner was dedicated to the yellow and grey Post Office colours and a computer system was installed to deal with letters, parcels, pensions, and so on. When you needed to collect a parcel or send a recorded letter, you just had to wait patiently by the counter until one of the supermarket staff became free from cashier or shelf re-stocking duties and attended to you. No problem. Just wait and someone would come and deal with your needs. What are five minutes in a life time? The Post Office franchise has now moved away from the supermarket and has gone to a convenience store across the road. The system is still the same, and postal services are mixed up with selling soft drinks, hiring out videos, and processing the lotto tickets. It seems to work.

It was a warm July day. Holiday time in Finland. It is when the population of the village triplicates with the influx of visitors spending time in their summer cottages by the infinity of lakes in the area. A few cars were parked by the two supermarkets. An air of soporific tranquillity prevailed.

The village seemed to have been planted by some socialistic planner with peculiar disregard for any resemblance of design or layout, in the middle of the beautiful countryside blessed by Lake Paijanne and by the myriad of other lakes around it.

Box-like buildings, typical of the 1950s, lined up the sides of the main road. Square concrete shapeless constructions such as can be found in most East European countries that have felt in various degrees the populist influence of the old Soviet Union. So many places we have seen, between Helsinki and Jyvaskyla, all suffer with the same ill-conceived and tasteless urbanistic schemes that were the fashion some fifty years ago and that completely neglected the need for harmony, shape or cultural traditions.

Our village was a typical example. Just an array of ugly, grey faceless buildings. I do not have anything against modern architecture, some expressions of which can no doubt be commended and can be found in almost every corner of the world, including of course in Finland. After all, Finland is the birthplace of some of the best-known designers and architects the world has seen. But the Fifties and Sixties, still quite close to World War II and with their desperate aspiration for popular reconstruction and relief, ought to be relegated to oblivion and never forgiven for producing some of the worst architectural monstrosities that are, unfortunately, still in existence.

As to our village, only a few hundred metres from the ugly and impersonal keskusta (centre) lies the lovely old original settlement, with its wooden houses in pastel colours, hugged together almost in an embrace to keep warm. One single road cutting it through, with Paijanne to the east and the South Lake to the west. (It makes sense, rest assured.) The old school, the old chemist and the old bakery are still standing and inhabited. It seems that the village is still begging for forgiveness for the ugly blocks only a short distance away.

In the village proper we walked into one of the supermarkets, and the atmosphere was the familiar one. Vegetables at the entrance, followed by a meat counter, and so on. The world has become the same all over – with one great difference: in our village supermarket there were no people and no music, just peace.

We were told that the village population consisted on some 3,000 souls—in winter. We soon learnt that when people talk about the village, they mean the district, the borough, the whole area falling under the village administration. As always in Finland, the concept of space is on a different scale if compared to most European countries. This means that if a "village" is made up of 3,000 inhabitants, only about 500 or 600 actually live in what you see as the village. The rest are scattered over a vast area of forests and woods, in small communities, each trying to maintain its own identity, each with its own Mayor or Mayoress; in times gone by this figure would have been the tribal chief, the strongest or the richest among the community. Each community has its own traditions and feasts. In fact what we perceive as the "village" is commonly referred to by locals as the "town", while the various hamlets making up the town borough are the individual villages.

The concept maintains the characters of the hunter-gatherer communities that first inhabited the forests and developed their own habits and rules, occasionally coming into contact with the neighbouring communities and often fighting them for the possession of the land and of the animals. The Laws, established by faraway rulers in large distant cities who did not understand life in the forest, were something to be generally ignored and never implemented.

Today the Laws are known and accepted and the village administration is in the hands of elected people in the town; but even so, the traditions and rituals of the individual villages or tribes are religiously maintained, almost as an anchor of safety and security.

During the summer months and on the occasional national holiday in winter, the village population triplicates, so we have been told, and we see new faces, newer cars, and new fashions in the local supermarkets. Visitors from Helsinki and the south, still in their city mode of rush and pompousness, appear and pretend to rule. Luckily, it does not take them long to fall back into the Finnish country lifestyle of casual clothes and slow pace, politeness, and patience. Sadly by then their holiday time is generally over, and they go back to their city lives, thankfully once again leaving the village to its true community.

Our village – I somehow cannot convince myself to call it a town – has a lovely harbour, once the busy little port for the comings and goings of an active paper mill. The mill is still standing, with its beautiful brick buildings and the tall chimney. No longer used as a mill, it could be turned into a museum like many of its equals in Finland or into some active recreation centre, preserving the lovely Victorian structure of the late ^{nineteenth} century and giving life to the village. It may still happen, if the local administration manages to find some sparkle and some money during one of the undoubtedly dreary meetings of the Council. I hope it does.

A few years ago, at long last, Alko decided to open a shop in the village. Alko is the state-controlled company that has the monopoly to sell spirits and make hefty profits from doing so. Finland is a heavy-drinking country. The long winter days, when the snow is thick on the ground and light is at a premium, make people drink. The endless bright summer days, with the sunshine at midnight and the wonderfully blue lake water, make people drink. The special days in the Finnish calendar, when celebrations are in order – be it Vappu (May 1, Workers' and Students' Day), Juhannus Day (June 24), or the glorious Midsummer's Day – make people drink... I have many times wondered about the accuracy of the booklet that we purchased prior to our first visit to Helsinki, in which it was stated that the country's national drink is coffee. No doubt a lot of coffee is drunk, always accompanied by biscuits or cakes, but also awfully large quantities of beer, vina, vodka and wine are consumed.

When we first arrived, our village did not have an Alko shop. This meant having to purchase spirits in the couple of local bars (that tend to continue selling alcohol to individuals even if they clearly show signs of heavy intoxication) or make quick trips to the nearby town with an Alko shop. We did this many a time when we realized that the bottle of whisky – used, of course, for medicinal purposes only – was coming to a sad end.

Then suddenly Alko appeared in the village next to a service station with plenty of parking space. It has brought revenue to the village, and it has increased the spending of the locals. I am told that our own village's Alko has now become the highest revenue point of sales for the company outside of Helsinki. We may have contributed in our small way, but it certainly speaks loads for the village life anyway.

The Language

Once we knew that for at least the following three years we would be spending some time in Finland, we bought in Foyle's a couple of Finnish grammar books for beginners and quite diligently we dedicated ourselves to learning some basic expressions and verbs. After all, we had lived abroad for some considerable time and had travelled quite a bit, never facing any serious problem in either mastering a language or at least in making ourselves understood by locals.

We would normally go through the grammar books in bed before sleeping as a kind of night time reading. During the day our minds were always busy with other things.

Bad idea. We found it difficult even to just get beyond the pages teaching the pronunciation of the letter "a", with its different sounds, described as "a like in apple", "a like in mad", or "a like in bus". (Well, I am talking about the sound, not the shape.)

We would soon be asleep, without even attempting to have a dream in Finnish. It was probably a reflection of our ageing brains no longer so prompt in absorbing new words. Or there could be a much simpler explanation: the Finnish language is a very difficult one.

Though it may seem very basic, with its lack of genders, pronouns, elaborate syntax, etc., it still maintains some fundamental aspects of Latin grammar, such as cases and phrase constructions. Even so, it appears to have no relevance whatsoever to any other language in the western world.

Years ago I spent long periods of time on a regular basis on business in Hungary and I recall someone telling me that Hungarian and Finnish are cousin languages, with great similarities with each other It may have been so when people conversed by sign language, but they certainly could not be more different now.

I would best describe Finnish as a kind of European Chinese - or Thai. Its origins are certainly in the east, particularly in the region of the Urals, from where the Finnish population originally migrated west. It was at a time when Hungarians and Finns marched together across the infinite plains of Russia towards the heart of Europe. Finns like to think that at a major junction somewhere – probably in Ukraine – they came across a sign with the word "Finland" pointing north, and only those who could read came to this country. It is something that Hungarians have always taken with a smile.

The truth of the matter is that the Finnish language did not exist as such and continued not to exist until the middle of the nineteenth century, when a gentleman by the name of J.V. Snellman, a philosopher and a sociologist from the Academy of Turku, founded his Saima newspaper in Finnish. Snellman dedicated his life to giving this country a unified language, in the full knowledge that without a common idiom, Finland might have continued to be a country but would never be a nation. His persistent belief was in fact that there cannot be a nation without a national language.

The majority of the population lived in small isolated communities scattered over a vast land of forests and lakes. People had no contact with the small nucleus of intellectuals – mostly monks – who tried to administer the country from Turku or Porvoo or (later) Helsinki and who used Latin or German or Swedish as official languages. The tribal communities had neither the means nor the desire to identify themselves with the city elites who could not understand either their dialects or their ways of life.

It was another intellectual by the name of Elias Lonnrot who, around the same time when Snellman published his first newspaper in Finnish, produced the first edition of the Kalevala and of the

Kantetelar, both considered as the epic tales of Finland. Lonnrot followed up the discoveries of Zacharia Topelius the elder and collected a massive amount of folk poetry and folk songs from Karelia, this historically all-important part of the Finnish territory which is so deeply rooted in Finnish tradition and in the hearts of the Finns. Karelia and its major city Viipuri had to be handed over to Russia after the Winter Wars and this is still today a very sore and painful subject for every Finn.

No doubt the mysterious and at times frightening epic tales of Kalevala and Kantetelar represent the very first example of Finnish literature. With them Lonnrot provided the people with the stepping stone towards the national identity that they so strongly needed.

Today's language is still young – less than 200 years of age – and is still developing into a unified national tongue out of the thousands of dialects that are still spoken all through the country. The result is that even when , after a struggle and a lot of bedtime reading of grammar books, we at last master a phrase and proudly use it, after learning it and trying to remember it, we are often told that in fact it is not really used in conversation that way. Usually, we are given a variety of alternative expressions which seem and sound completely different from what we have learnt, much to our disappointment and amusement.

Also our village also has of course its own peculiar dialect of course, and often we have found that the modern written official language or even the instruction leaflets on some products cannot be fully understood by some of the older villagers.

For some 600 years Finland was under Swedish rule. It was a province of the Kingdom of Sweden, which exploited the natural resources of the land and used it as a hunting ground for the nobility. Swedish was the official language of the cultural centres, especially Turku and the south-western coastal towns, but it was never accepted or absorbed by the population at large. It was the language of invaders and occupants, of people who really did not understand the life and the habits of the scattered communities.

When Finland was handed over by Sweden to Czar Alexander in 1809, like a plate of biscuits, the country became an extension of the Russian Empire and the new masters tried to impose Russian as the official language, once again neglecting the fact that people in the forests did not care about Russian and did not need or want to speak it. Russian elites spoke French anyway and the Czar had no interest in "colonizing" Finland or in spending his money to educate the Finns in Russian ways. He was only interested in hunting and in the advantage of using a couple of ports in the Gulf of Finland from where he could sail off with his family from St Petersburg to European ports.

Swedish is still studied today at school as a second "mother tongue", although an increasing number of students are abandoning it after a few years. Fewer and fewer of the new generations are fluent in Swedish and an increasing number of people are against speaking it. As to Russian, it was a compulsory subject in schools until the World War II, and a whole generation of Finns did in fact learn it, but refused point blank to speak it. Not many young Finns speak Russian today.

Finnish is of course the nation's language, but it is still early days. It is, for example, surprising that despite the efforts by Snellman and Lonnrot one hundred years earlier, even as late as the middle of the last century we find General Mannerheim – war hero and one of the presidents of Finland – speaking Swedish or French to his soldiers during the Winter Wars, because his knowledge and estimation of the Finnish language were so poor.

In conclusion, our first encounter with the spoken language was, to say the least, depressing.

It is a language made of impossibly long words, often with an unimaginable number of consonants and double letters with which over the years we have become slightly more familiar, despite the fact that our vocabulary is still very limited and our grammar poor. But it is a language that fascinates us and that makes us jump for joy whenever we manage to just put a sentence together or capture the sense of what others say to us. It is rewarding to see the genuine appreciation on people's faces when we express ourselves in Finnish. "Astonishing", a friend said to us when she and her husband were telling us the prices of some building materials (in English) and we repeated the figures in Finnish, apparently with an even tolerable accent.

After a good number of years, we have begun to make some sense of the way the words are constructed in order to give them meanings by combining terms together. Adding the famous endings they identify direction and possession. Even here, however, a lot is left to almost personal inventiveness, and often the root of the word is altered for no apparent reason before an ending is attached to it. It seems that the exceptions are almost more frequent than the rules, to the complete dismay and discouragement of the poor and, in our case, old language students.

Luckily for us, English has become the country's second language and a good seventy per cent of the people we have come across speak it. It has made our life easier in every respect. The Finns' command of English is as impressive, as much as their appreciation and understanding of the English sense of humour. The invasion of English TV programs, which are avidly watched, and the Finn's ability to capture both vocabulary and meanings result in an astounding level of fluency.

I recall one evening when Paula and Tuomo invited us for a coffee and some cakes at their new home in the forest. The conversation flowed in English, covering a variety of subjects, but excluding politics, something that Finns do not care too much about. For reasons that I now forget the English expression "hanky panky" was used by Celia, and inevitably its light-hearted and naughty meaning had to be explained. In any language, explanations always take the impact, the drama, or the comedy out of phrases or jokes, and the subject was soon dropped. When it was time to leave, we thanked out hosts for the pleasant evening and jokingly pointed out that we did not want to overstay our welcome. Tuomo, with his typically straight face, said, "Well, I feel some hanky panky coming up anyway."

On the other hand, sometimes when trying to be formal and perfect, things get "lost in translation", like when we read the instruction leaflet for an electrical implement we had bought. The text was provided in several languages, including English. The translator must have been feeling merry when at the end of the instructions he or she added some word of warning about the use of the equipment: "Beware of children." Blessed be that translator, and may the children show forgiveness!

Not very long ago my car developed a little problem. (You always hope that your car's problems are little and that you can continue to drive it, usually with the conviction that the problem will disappear on its own). I booked it in with Seppo. Seppo is one of the two car mechanics in the village. Heikki is the other. Their workshops are opposite each other on either side of a major road going north out of the village. They seem to have divided their expertise and equipment, and together they cover all the needs of the local drivers. Seppo is a hands-on kind of mechanic, with painting and body-work facilities, a slightly overcrowded workshop, a sense for inventiveness, and frontier solutions to problems. Heikki has an immaculate workshop, tyre-changing equipment, and a little shop selling accessories and parts. He even wears plastic gloves when working. They are both very nice and helpful and do not seem to compete with each other but rather to complement each other.

I drove to see Seppo and he decided that he needed about half an hour to solve my car problem. So he booked it for the following day at 9.00.

Having learnt from the Finns how fundamental punctuality is, I was at the workshop on time. The door was still locked, and Seppo's van was not in the drive. I waited, expecting to see him appear at any moment. Five minutes later I decided that the delay was too abnormal for a Finn and I called Seppo's mobile telephone. He answered and apologized profusely for the delay, stating that he would be with me in a few minutes. "I am so sorry, I am eating my son," he added. I knew that he had recently become the father of a little boy, and I smiled silently, imagining Seppo, the dedicated father, eating a limb off the poor boy. The truth was that Seppo was actually feeding his son, of course – a wonderfully colourful image, somewhat distorted by the translation; amusing, candid, and sweet. I almost wish we could make the same wonderful mistakes in Finnish, but our knowledge is too poor even to be just amusing.

We do sincerely appreciate the fact that in Finland we can do anything and everything in English. This is a country where bank statements are provided in English if the customer is English-speaking, where telephone bills are itemised in English if they are addressed to an English-speaking user and where all public offices have telephone help lines in English. Even at market stalls we can buy freshly picked potatoes and cauliflowers and be addressed in English, once our efforts to express ourselves in Finnish have obviously resulted in comic disaster.

It is also a proof of the Finns' determination to feel and become part of the western world, after years of fencing between East and West without a precise identity. The difficult balancing act conducted by the famous hard-line President Kekkonen, who turned his back on Russia without bowing to the West, is long gone. Finland has joined Europe and, as in everything else, it has done it so seriously and totally. The Finnish language, spoken only by Finns, would severely limit the development of its international image. Pragmatically and realistically, Finland is giving its new generations the opportunity to feel part of the world but at the same time maintain their feet firmly on the nation's ground, made of forests and traditions. It is a healthy and safe compromise that would make even Lonnrot and Snellman happy.

Shopping

Even before going into one of the village supermarkets, we decided to pay a visit to the electrical shop. It seemed to have everything, from television sets to light bulbs, from dishwashers to electric fans and air conditioners. It also sold boats, lovely green fibreglass boats with or without electric engines, and bicycles.

We had decided that we needed an electric kettle for our morning tea and for our coffees. Coffee in Finland is always brewed in a percolator and served in small cups, generally nicely presented with a paper napkin through the cup handle and with a small spoon, used to stir the sugar or the milk in the coffee but also to eat the cakes that are always served with it. No Finn would ever dream of drinking coffee on its own, no matter what time of the day. Biscuits or pula (a bun-type sweet roll) or cakes – when coffee is served more formally in the afternoon if friends come and visit - always accompany coffee. And it is just never drank while standing up but always taking time for a short break and a bit of relaxation, resting on a chair or a stool or simply on a house wooden step.

As I mentioned earlier, I had read in my booklet on Finland prior to our very first visit to Helsinki that coffee is considered the national drink. I mean non-alcoholic drink of course. When it comes to alcohol, vodka and vina and beer are far ahead of coffee. In the past we lived many years in Italy, where coffee is brewed in the traditional Neapolitan percolator, but only after this has been used a number of times and its contents have been religiously thrown away on each occasion so that the steel flavour has disappeared from it and does not contaminate the aroma of the coffee. All the same we have become accustomed to the more practical habit of drinking instant coffee, which means a quicker preparation and less washing up, and, quite frankly, the taste is okay, at least for our palates that are not so sophisticated as the Italians claim to have.

Also some of our friends in Finland have now taken up the concept of instant coffee, after a few doubts, which they now seem to consider a wonderful innovation on the old tradition. Some have even gone to the extreme of declaring that instant coffee is quite good, although still avoiding the subject in front of the older generation of Finns, who would maintain with no compromise that this bastardisation of "the" real coffee is not worth drinking. Slowly old habits are changing, even in a country that is so strongly clinging to its traditions. Jars of Nescafe are now in every supermarket.

So we decided we needed a kettle.

An elderly lady was in the shop talking to a pleasant young woman, who turned out to be the shop owner and who later became, with her husband, a friend of ours. The elderly lady was clearly in need of a light bulb—that we could tell for sure, even with our non-existent knowledge of Finnish. She was holding the light bulb up to the shop window and looking at it against the sun, apparently inquiring about the shape of the bulb, the solidity of the glass, and the power of its filament.

A few times the bulb was put down on the counter and other bulbs were examined and discussed, seemingly with the same precision. Irja, the shop owner, gave the elderly lady all the required explanations, with no sign of impatience or discomfort at the sight of other potential customers having walked through the door. After about fifteen minutes the elderly lady purchased her light bulb and walked out, satisfied and confident to have made the right choice. Irja then came to dedicate her time to us.

It was our first encounter with Finnish shopping methods.

The elderly lady probably lived alone in a small cottage in the forest, surrounded by berries and fir trees and hare and elks and maybe bears. Probably she had no opportunity of seeing her neighbours for weeks, especially during the long winter days and dark nights. Irja's friendly face was all she needed to have a chat and be reassured that she was not alone. The bulb might have been an excuse. Or probably she was just the typical example of a Finnish person having to decide on her own what to purchase. And that is always difficult.

In an empty country, where cottages and houses are scattered over a vast wooded land and the daily contact with other human beings is not so frequent, the inner sense of insecurity and the general fear of having to make decisions are reflected in the shopping culture. The old adage "safety in numbers" is proven wise in Finland. People are so few and so far from one another that inevitably they do not feel safe or confident about their ways unless someone gives them reassurance that they are the right ways. Purchasing an item, of whatever nature, represents a scary dilemma, unless friends, relatives, neighbours, or even the shop assistant convince them that the item is right and adequate for the task. It is the heritage of a young country which is still trying to find its roots after centuries of being used as a playing field by foreign powers and after decades of hesitation between East and West. No decision is to be made hurriedly – or alone.

Whatever the reason, the lady walked out of the shop as a satisfied customer and from that day we have always remembered that when we shop in Finland, there is never any need for impatience or hurry. When our turn comes we can rest assured of the total attention of the assistant for as long as it takes, just as the customer before us and the customer after us. Everyone waits, with no grunting, puffing or moaning.

Years after that first summer in Finland, we needed to buy a wheelbarrow. The old yellow and red one that Juhani had left for us to use in the garden was seriously old and rusty. We went into a large hardware store in the nearby town, and in a matter of minutes came out with a brand-new zinc wheelbarrow with dark green aluminium frame and red handles – and a wheel of course.

A few days later we were invited for dinner by Pirkko and Eino, some very good friends, who of course live in a lovely red wood house in the forest. I happened to mention with pride that we had managed to buy a new wheelbarrow even with our limited Finnish vocabulary. I shall never forget the expression of disappointment and total surprise on our friends' faces at the fact that we had made the purchase without consulting them or anyone else before deciding. They explained that a purchase of that nature is never done by Finns without first inquiring with at least three different people as to the quality, the efficiency, the durability, and the design of the item involved. And when my reaction was "Well, a wheelbarrow is only a wheelbarrow after all. As long as it has a wheel and a barrow, it is fine," our friends were genuinely puzzled. They thought we were rather unique in our speed at making decisions.

We are back to the question of communicating with others. It was not so much that we had purchased a wheelbarrow on our own and quickly. The amazing thing was that we had not talked to anyone about it.

I could mention innumerable examples of this shopping culture that seems to be typical of all Finns and relates to all possible items, be they complicated mechanical instruments or simple everyday products. One case that comes to my mind happened very recently in the same hardware store where I dared to buy the wheelbarrow. (I am sure that the shop assistants try to hide whenever I walk through the door.) I needed some nails and I waited while the assistant was with another customer, who was apparently in need of an extendable tape measure, one of those thin metal things with lines one centimetre apart that have a kind of hook at one end so that you can fix it against an edge or in a crevice and pull the tape all the way along the distance you wish to measure and that, just at the last moment when you are almost ready to make a mark with your pencil by the correct measurement, spring back so that you have to start all over again.

The customer was standing by a rack with about half a dozen of such extendable tapes and was closely examining each and every one of them. Each tape was pulled out about thirty centimetres and then let loose to spring back into its casing. The weight of each item was assessed. Probably the colour was also assessed. Again the tape was pulled out. It was examined on each side (the marks and the numbers are always only on one side) and the opinion of the shop assistant was sought each time, as if different tapes had centimetres of different lengths.

In the end the assistant came to me while the gentleman was still examining all the items on the rack, and I bought my nails. I have no idea what happened to the other customer or whether he finally decided that it might be more prudent measuring whatever he had to measure by using hands and thumbs. Maybe he had nightmares about the fact that some extendable tapes even here in Finland show both centimetres and inches. This added option must have caused some very serious dilemma and possibly a nervous breakdown. I never saw him again.

We know the system only too well by now. When we enter a shop and find someone there before us, we know that we will be there for a long time. Whatever the item, when a Finn has to buy something, the decisional process is never fast and the conversation with the shop assistant always takes on the colours of a pantomime, but everything is done in genuinely good spirit and with the honest intention on the assistants' part to help and assist the customer

Recently I went to the local hardware shop. (Believe it or not, I do not actually spend my whole life in hardware shops.) It is a large and well-stocked store that sells pretty much everything under the sun, (with the exception of food), including compost and fertilizers. We had thought of buying some fertilizer for some of our younger trees in order to help them get through winter. Armed with memories of English garden centres, I asked the assistant for some bags of the most suitable food for conifer trees. Simple enough, I thought.

After a few minutes of humming and scratching his head, he noticed that another person had walked into the shop, whose English was superior to his own, and he went for help. In fact I knew the person myself very well, since he was the local computer expert who had rescued me on several occasions when the laptop decided to develop a brain of its own or to go on strike. A convoluted conversation then started between the computer expert and the shop assistant, while we were all standing by a pallet of bags of what looked to me just the fertilizer I needed.

Occasionally breaking their intense exchange in Finnish to ask me questions as to the type of trees, their height, their position in the garden, their colour, and so on, the two went on discussing the complicated subject for some ten minutes, at which point a local handyman arrived and found himself becoming involved in the "board meeting" about my fertilizer. Another ten minutes went by, the three of them examining the instructions on the bags relating to the quantity of water to be mixed with so much fertilizer, the temperature of the soil, and probably the angle of the moon compared to the sun at the time of use. I was only a spectator.

Finally the verdict was delivered. "We think that this is okay." So I bought a couple of bags. I had been shopping in a Finnish village store, and everyone had done his best to assist me. The wonderful thing is that everything was done with a genuine and sincere desire to help on the part of the computer expert, the shop assistant, and the handyman. This is what makes Finns so delightful and pleasant – and maybe so slow in deciding. They are truly wonderful people.

Another amusing example is more recent. I walked into a clothes store in the nearby town with the intention of buying a cardigan. I like cardigans. I find them comfortable and easy, both at home and out. If it is cold the buttons can be done up and if it is warm they can be undone to make the cardigan casual and relaxing.

I found something I liked, but unfortunately not in the right size or colour. Very kindly, the lady who runs the store offered to order me one in the right size and colour from the manufacturer's wholesaler and was immediately on the phone having an elaborate discussion with someone about my cardigan at the end of which, she informed me that the item would be despatched the following day and it would be in the store within a couple of days.

Aware of the Finnish precision when it comes to timing, I went back to the store three days later, only to be informed by the same lady, with a very disappointed and sad expression on her face, that the cardigan should have arrived the day before but it had not. She called the wholesaler again and undoubtedly told them off – although her expression never changed – and in the end she asked me to return within an hour when she would have the item. I did so, but the item was still not there. I pointed out that it would not be possible for me to come back to the store until our next visit to Finland as we would be leaving in three days. We arranged that as soon as the cardigan would be received in the store, the lady would post it to me. There was no need to pay for it in advance, as she would insert a bank credit slip for me to pay upon receipt.

The following I was called at home and informed that the cardigan had actually arrived. So as not to delay it any further, she would hand it over to the driver of the bus that regularly travels between our village and the little town, and I would be able to pick the parcel up at the bus station. I would be called by someone from the bus station to let me know that a parcel was waiting for me. No more than ten minutes later, I was called again by the store lady who informed me that a client was in the store at that moment and would be driving back to our village very shortly. She planned to hand the small parcel to her client, and this unknown person would leave it at the service station at the entrance to our village. In that way I would be able to have my cardigan within an hour. I was puzzled.

When I walked into the service station, preparing in my mind a suitable phrase in Finnish to explain my case, the girl behind the counter, at which people can pay for food, petrol, fishing articles and life jackets, looked at me and immediately handed me the little parcel with my cardigan that had been kept on a shelf waiting for me. I did not have to say a word or pay anything. That is just the beauty of Finnish service and efficiency.

One day we had been buying the usual food and grocery products in one of the supermarkets. It looked the same as any other supermarket in the world, except that the shoppers were very few and very quiet and that we never heard any announcement through the tannoy system requesting in a plastic voice that "Miss Fletcher come to customer service at once." We happened to be walking out, pushing our full trolley, at the same time as an elderly couple. The man was in front, carrying nothing; one hand casually in his pocket as he went leisurely to his car. The lady – presumably his wife – was following him carrying two full bags in one hand and a crate of beer in the other, like an obedient workhorse. At one point the poor woman almost dropped the crate of beer just as she was crossing the road, and like a Good Samaritan I rescued her and helped her over the last few steps to the car. She never stopped thanking me, almost bowing in gratitude and surprise. The man had not even noticed. Nor did he pay any attention to the woman when she opened the car boot to load the shopping. He just sat in the car waiting for the woman to climb in. After all, he had done his good deed and taken the woman shopping.

Shopping in Finland is no doubt a far cry from what we have been used to and even after the shopping is done, the attitude of people here is so different! One amusing aspect is the way everyone is keen to know the price of the goods you buy.

In England this is the apex of rudeness, an interference into personal privacy. Only when it comes to properties do the English suddenly become willing to reveal prices, mortgages, interest rates, etc. It seems that letting you know how much they paid for their houses gives a sense of wealth that they are eager to reveal even to strangers. And then they say, "Our mortgage was so-and-so some twenty-five years ago, so you can imagine what it would be like today with the increase in value." Then they pause, waiting for you to open your mouth in admiration and surprise, hoping to impress you and wanting to feel richer than you. Only when you have fallen into the trap and expressed some form of astonishment at how wealthy your friend must be, does the typical English fake understatement emerge and you hear, "But it was not too difficult, you know," pouring salt on your wound.

However, when the item in question is instead a simple object that you may have bought in a hardware store or in a shopping precinct, never would the English dare expose their curiosity and ask you for its price and never would you dream of attempting to give the price away.

We were therefore rather taken aback when we told some friends that we had found something – I have now forgotten what it was - that would be ideal for our kitchen, and we were asked, "Was it expensive? How much was it?" The horror on our English faces must have been just about concealed under a cold smile and under the typically non-committal reply, "It was not too bad." We thought our friends had behaved in a totally unacceptable manner and probably needed a lesson in etiquette, but when the incident happened again and again, with different people and different products, we began to suspect that maybe we were missing something, part of the understanding of a country where most things are still down to basics, without silly complexes and mannerisms. People here are simply and candidly curious and want to make conversation about what you have bought. There is no jealousy or desire to copy you. After all, everything has a price, so what is the secrecy about?

We have got used to it now, and we have ourselves started inquiring about the cost of items purchased by our friends. By doing so, we feel strangely closer to being Finnish – sadly apart from the language, of course.

The Russian Neighbour

Finland has almost 1,500 kilometres of border with Russia. The two countries have been neighbours for ever, and for one and a half centuries Finland was a province of Czar Nicolai's Russia and of Stalin's Soviet Union.

Constantly attracted by the trading advantages offered by the West and constantly frightened to upset its powerful eastern neighbour, Finland has lived a difficult and uncertain past that has heavily contributed to its still evident – and now totally unjustified – insecurity. I say "totally unjustified" in the light of the country's technological achievements and of the respect that this small nation now enjoys on the world scene.

There is not a lot of love lost between Finland and its neighbour. After all, the Soviets took away Karelia at the end of the 1940 Winter Wars, despite the incredible resistance put up by the Finns who at times with their small units of troops well trained in snow and forest fighting, gave a good beating to the gigantic Bolshevik army machine. In the end the Finns had to succumb to the sheer numerical advantage of the enemy and had to painfully release the isthmus of Karelia and half Lake Ladoga, that vast expanse of water where many a Soviet tank miserably sank, probably unable to recognise the difference between fields and the frozen water when both were covered in snow.

Karelia is embedded in the heart of every Finn as the most traditional of the Finnish regions, where the Kalevala and the Kantetelar come from, with their epic tales of ancient tragedies and heroism. We have come across many people who moved from Karelia after the Winter Wars; in some cases, they even transported their houses by every conceivable means and relocated them away from the invaders, often on the western side of Lake Paijanne, which with its elongated shape seemed to offer a kind of protecting dam. The houses are still there, with their wooden structures, wonderful examples of the determination of people who wanted to remain free and Finnish. Karelians look different from the image that we may have of Finns. They tend to be shorter, stocky in build, rugged from centuries of hardship and weather extremes, closer to the Ural populations than to the Nordic genes. They are strong, determined, and proud, often with a sad look in their eyes that have longed for decades to see their beloved Karelia return under the Finnish Flag.

Russia and the Russians have always been the traditional enemies. Even nowadays in the perception of many Finns of the older generation – especially in the country - all bad things that appear in their country are the product of Russia – bears, soppi (a chunky-looking dog-like creature), wolves, prostitutes, illegal workers, rich fur-coated ladies in expensive four-wheel drives, and bad weather. They are all believed to cross over the border by Lappenranta and Imatra and take away pieces of this green and empty land. We must not forget that when the reprehensible tragedy of Chernobyl happened in 1986, the intricate system of air currents around our planet pushed most of the polluted and radioactive ashes and fumes from the smouldering Ukrainian plant on to Finland (and by strange coincidence particularly on Central Finland).

It is no wonder that the big neighbour has a good dose of unpopularity among the Finns.

We have ourselves experienced a few direct examples of the inhospitable attitude openly shown to Russian visitors (and there are many, especially in winter). On some occasions in shops we have surprisingly been mistaken for Russians, who in most cases speak to Finns in very good English. We received a kind of service that was very far from what we had been accustomed to and that lacked the Finns' usual politeness. Gone were the pleasantries and the helpful approach typically used towards both Finns and visitors, and in their place came cool unfriendly disinterest and dismissal. That was until we found a way to make it obvious that we in fact were English and managed to clear the misunderstanding. Back came the friendliness and the smile. And there is no doubt that when a Finn gives you the proverbial cold shoulder, the temperature is certainly sub-zero!

Kekkonen, the famous President of Finland of the post-war period, was the first to try to achieve a successful balancing act for his country between East and West. "Bowing too much to the West," he used to claim, "we just open our behind to the East." The border between the two countries runs for over a thousand kilometres, and this has always been seen as a kind of delicate area by the Finns, in the full consciousness that if Kekkonen's words are forgotten, the pressure from that direction would become difficult to contain.

It has been a difficult and often painful "fence" position for Finland, despite long-standing economic agreements with their neighbour, especially with regard to the supply of energy, most of which comes from Russia. When we visited Imatra for the first time, it was explained to us that by an unusual arrangement the dam on the river Vuoksi is opened at regular intervals so as to provide water for Russian power stations across the border, which in turn produce energy that is sold back to Finland.

Whatever the origin of the new Russian affluence may be, affluence it is. It is always shown with great arrogance and bad taste and almost with a kind of colonial approach to Finland. The best stores in Helsinki and the southern cities are regularly invaded by ostentatiously elegant Russian ladies, with their noses up in the air and their stocky husbands in tow. They walk around with the latest mobile technology clearly on show, as if they own the earth they stand on, ignoring shop assistants and throwing around the weight of their cash. "Yes, "said the manageress of one shop when we remarked at the number of Russian visitors in the Finnish capital, "and they come with brain-not-included." This may be a cruel and harsh comment in view of the amount of money that the Russians spend in the stores and that is welcomed by the Finnish economy, but unfortunately it reflects a fairly widespread sentiment.

In winter the Russian invasion is even more visible, this time coated in furs and designer boots. Often driving in convoys of the latest four-wheel drive vehicles, they swerve all over the roads and smoke everywhere. Despite the cold temperature, the ladies' noses are still stuck up in the air, and their elegance is decadent. They are nouveaux riches. Maybe in a few hundred years they will have managed to really look stylish.

Some Russian landmarks have been kept in Finland and have become famous, like the Valtionhotelly in Imatra, a rather gloomy and imposing stone construction that was regularly used by Russian dignitaries for their meetings. Imatra is only about six or seven kilometres from the nearest Russian town, and the hotel offered comfort and privacy for the comrades behind its thick walls. We had a coffee at the Valtionhotelly, served in a spacious and elegant room, while a wedding party was held in the next room. It was pleasant and relaxed, but the gloomy Bolshevik atmosphere seemed to be still there.

Another landmark is the Venajanlinna Hotel, on the edges of Hameenlinna. Situated by the shore of what is considered a purifying lake, the hotel had been transformed from its origin as a school for KGB agents into a luxurious and comfortable accommodation by a golf course. It is imposing, built from dark-red bricks, with a number of outbuildings that shelter the view of the pretty lake. We visited it with some friends and had a drink on the patio facing the lake at the end of the very well-kept gardens. It was peaceful and nice and someone even told us with pride that one of the Finnish Formula One world champions had got married there. That piece of news was probably supposed to make us feel good. It did not, really.

So Russia and Russian things are inevitably part of Finnish life, whether Finns like it or not. It is not all bad.

In the south-eastern corner of Finland, along the edges of Lake Saimaa and further south towards Imatra and Lappeenranta, small communities of Russians dot the countryside. They settled in Finland in the early part of the last century, escaping Lenin's revolution. They came with their few possessions, and they still maintain the peasants' simple culture and habits in their colourful wooden houses with clever carvings over windows and doors. Some of their monks and priests came with them too, founding monasteries and convents that maintain the spiritual unity that Lenin had tried to break in their country.

We visited a couple of these holy places, at Valamo and Lintula. Valamo is a large development with old and new buildings. It has been transformed by the Orthodox Monks into a pilgrimage destination; with a difference. From the small original settlement, it has now grown into a substantial business enterprise with its own restaurant that can serve hundreds of people, a mini supermarket selling locally produced wines and a variety of icons and souvenirs, and holiday cottages. When we visited it with some friends, it must have been one of the hottest days in that particular summer and the place was dry, dusty, and uncomfortable. The trees seemed recently planted and not as yet tall enough to offer any welcome shade. It did not feel very holy.

When we parked our car, a rather pompous lady approached us with some firm instruction as to the allowed attire and behaviour while on the holy ground. The tour of us felt like small children being put to a kind of test. I did not like her.

After a walk under the beating sun through the buildings - old and new - and a lunch in the large dining hall that would have fitted very well on the Costa del Sol, I had a brief talk with one of the young monks. He explained to me that the number of religious students in Valamo is in constant decline and the Order is finding it difficult to ensure a future for the monastery. I also suspect that the original Orthodox community is becoming smaller as the new generations melt away into a predominantly Lutheran society and inevitably forget their ancestral religious roots.

Lintula is very different. It is a convent where a small number of Orthodox nuns move quietly, pray, and make jams, bread and candles. The religious feeling is prevalent, and visitors feel compelled to walk slowly and in silence. Even the coffee shop, where a young nun serves you soft drinks and home-baked cakes with a candid smile, is calm and relaxed. The whole place permeates peace and serenity, with the low buildings that are dormitories to the nuns, immersed in fields and trees.

Between the two, I certainly felt better at Lintula. I am sure that God feels that way too.

Russians have recently started to invest a fair amount of money in Finnish properties and many have purchased cottages around Paijanne. The beauty and size of the lake and the relatively short distance from St Petersburg make it a convenient location. Finns may not like the fact that their land is being purchased by the old enemy, but they are intelligent and pragmatic enough to accept that the country needs tax-paying inhabitants and relies on Russian energy. If Moscow were to turn the switch off, Finland would be cold, dark and poor. It is a love-hate relationship that will probably never change.

We saw wooden observation towers along the old Karelian road, just out of Imatra, on either side of the border that occasionally runs through water. They are empty now and just stand as reminders of days gone by when soldiers from the two armies watched one another at gun point. The cold war is over, but the memories are still very much alive and maybe the TV programs showing films in Russian are doing a good job to keep them alive.

What is it they say? "The wolf (in this case the bear) may lose his fur but not its habits." It is always better to be aware.

The day when Finland finally became free from the Russian yoke, just over ninety years ago, is still celebrated as a national holiday. It was on December 6th 1917. In fact it was actually on November 30th that the Finnish Senate endorsed the document that had previously been approved by Lenin, granting Finland its freedom from the Soviets. The content of that famous and most important piece of paper was then implemented and put into place five weeks later.

We happened to be in Finland on November 30th 2007, and we were asked by a dear friend to join her at a ceremony of celebration and remembrance that would take place somewhere in the woods, not too far from us.

Aulikki picked us up in the afternoon and drove very slowly the fifty kilometres to a turning that pointed to nowhere. It was raining, and by that time it was dark, a miserable night such as you always get in the Finnish country in winter when snow is not yet on the ground. Everything was black, and the narrow track winding its way through the forest looked precarious and slippery, suited for a rally competition rather than for Aulikki's timid driving skills that do not contemplate gear changing as frequently as bends require. Despite her strong four-wheel-drive vehicle, on quite a few occasions I did have visions of us catapulting into a ditch or ending up against a tree.

When we finally arrived at our destination, we saw a small wooden hut in an opening of the forest. Some military personnel were guiding the cars to suitable parking places in the mud. Smoke was puffing out of a white van through a metal pipe where some food was being cooked. The whole place looked surreal.

Inside the hut several people in casual winter clothes were sitting round wooden tables, squeezed almost against the walls to make room for everyone. The characters seemed to have stepped out of an old Bible or out of a Lord of the Rings episode. We saw bearded, stern faces, forest clothing, serious and intimidating looks.

We walked in, introducing ourselves to everyone in the usual Finnish fashion, and we sat in a kind of second room, where a makeshift altar had been prepared by the air force colonel and chaplain who would officiate the simple remembrance and Holy Communion service. When he was told that we came from England he apologised for the fact that he had not received any advance notification and had not prepared any address in English. We felt welcome and part of a very special and dedicated community.

The service comprised a small speech and a reading from the Testament, which I was pleased to be able to partially understand. The focus was on the liberation of this small nation from the Russian hold and on the sacrifices made by the Finns to ensure that freedom could be maintained. Central Finland was the scene of some of the worst and bloodiest battles between the Reds and the Whites, and many lives were lost in the civil war that for a period of time divided the country.

After Communion, large plastic bowls of hot vegetable and pork soup were served, each with a paper bag containing rye bread and butter. The soup was comforting, rich in flavour, and warming.

When we left, I was dreading the drive back along the winding forest track and hoping that other cars ahead of us would slow Aulikki enough for us to get safely to the main road, where her speed would again be reduced to an almost ridiculous – but safe – level. She and her husband Heikki are among our best friends and I am sure that she will not be offended by my comments about her driving. After all, she only managed to flatten a few orange plastic poles that had been fixed into the ground along the edges of our own drive – to help the snowplough clear only the necessary spaces – when she came to visit us once in winter and had to reverse and park the car.

We had enjoyed a bizarre and interesting evening and we had felt completely absorbed by this simple and sincere society – all thanks to the Russians, who gave Finland its freedom some ninety years ago.

The Swedish Neighbour

Russia to the east and Sweden to the west. Two vastly different countries. Two vastly different owners of Finland's history.

The Swedish Crown possessed Finland (or better the land where Finland is now) for almost 600 years until the eighteenth century A short sailing trip across the Gulf of Bothnia made it easy for the Swedes to come over and hunt, as well as establish some living communities that immediately led them to feel that they were the owners and managers of this vast empty country.

Sweden is a large and empty country itself and the attraction for the sailors and pilgrims to cross the water and reach the shores of Finland was simply an interest in the unknown rather than necessity dictated by the search for food. Once on Finnish land they generally did not go very far and did not find it difficult to settle, mostly on the western and south-western coast. They were not conquerors, but rather explorers travelling under the Swedish flag who just managed to find some extra hunting land. Some decided to stay and enjoy the richness of the forests, the abundance of berries and fish and the space available to them. So Finland became a Grand Duchy of Sweden with Swedish legislators and Governors.

Turku (or Abo in Swedish) was the first capital city. A largish town with an ancient cathedral and an imposing stone castle, close to the shore, it enjoyed the rewards and the pleasures of any city crossed by a river. It was possible for merchants and traders to come by sea and reach the central cobbled stone square by the cathedral to sell their produce in old markets set up by its walls. In the same square today the Declaration of Peace is still read every Christmas Eve by the Mayor of Turku, from the balcony of the public administration building at exactly 12.00 noon. It is read in both Finnish and Swedish, and it marks the official beginning of the Christmas festivities. The Declaration, originally written by an unknown priest in the seventeenth century, is a short, simple document that some friends have translated for us and have written on a rolled-up sheet with a ribbon around it. It just wishes peace and happiness to the nation. Most of Finland watches the event every year on television, and the Turku Cathedral Square is always packed with families instilling in their children the importance of tradition and respect, something that so many nations have now forgotten.

Since the first skeleton of administration was Swedish, the official language was inevitably Swedish. Swedish is a harsh rather guttural language that appears to need a stern face and a limited sense of humour to be spoken correctly and that the Turku administrators tried with little success to impose on the Finns. These natives would not have cared too much about the legislation that Turku put on paper and that it had no way to impose. The forests had their own laws and they had no contacts or connection with the written documents that nobody could understand anyway. The influence of the Church and of the monks who found the courage and the stamina to travel to Finland was much more perceived as a kind of unifying message than the abstract and distant regulations of the Swedish Masters. The monks actually lived within the small communities, and they better understood their way of life, aspirations, and needs.

So Finland continued to be just a hunting ground for the Swedes. There are debates about the number of times that the Swedish Kings visited Finland whilst it was one of their provinces. It was probably very few times, if any. Finland was simply a Grand Duchy of Sweden, an appendix attached to the kingdom by a thin piece of land, very much up north, where perennial winter reigned and the mountains became high and impassable. The Swedish language was the language of the elites, the learned and the law. It was not the language of the people.

And so it stayed until the Swedish Crown came to an arrangement with the Russian Czar in the nineteenth century. Under this agreement, the Grand Duchy of Finland would be "sold" to Russia, giving the eastern neighbour access to hunting, as well to ports closer to the North Sea.

Even after Lonroth's and Snellman's historical successes in creating a national language for Finland, Swedish still remained the basic language to be taught in school. The Russians tried with no enthusiasm or conviction to make their language accepted and embraced by Finns, but it turned out to be a completely wasted exercise. Even today, Swedish is taught in schools, but despite the fact that most middle-aged Finns are able to speak Swedish, it has been slowly replaced by English as the second main language. (This is, of course, much to our personal delight, simply because in our old age we feel less need to remember difficult expressions that would impose too much pressure on our tired brains.) Some people even openly object to speaking Swedish, remembering the 600 years of domination by their western neighbour. The young people simply are not interested in learning Swedish; all they want to remember about Sweden is Abba, the pop group from the seventies, although the Swedish Royal Family is among the most respected institutions and some of their family members (including the Queen) are extremely handsome.

I recall when a few years ago a couple of good friends – actually our opposite neighbours in England – came to spend two weeks in Finland and stayed at our cottage in the woods. It was early March, and the weather had put up its best suit. There was plenty of fluffy dry snow, temperatures around minus 20 Celsius, clear blue skies, and sunshine.

Our friends are a mixed couple, in as much Cecilia is Swedish and her husband John is English with some Swedish blood in his veins from past generations. They are both fluent in Swedish. Remembering the past association between Finland and Sweden, they tried – probably as a way to make themselves accepted by locals – to talk Swedish to people.

One day they decided to buy some fish from our neighbour, and I walked with them over to the shed where Jorma keeps his freshly caught stock of perch, pike-perch, white fish, salmon, and the like.

When they saw Jorma come towards them they greeted him in Swedish and I believe they asked him if they could buy some fish from him. He replied to the salutations in Finnish, and then he turned to me, expecting me to explain in English what these people wanted. I am sure that Jorma, who is now in his late fifties, knows and speaks Swedish reasonably well, having learnt it at school in the years when the language was compulsory, but he would not say a word in that language. I felt as if I had introduced some invaders to him. It may be that many here feel like that.

There are definite similarities between Finland and its former owner. The climate is similar, although a good chunk of Sweden is considerably further south than the Finnish coastline in the Gulf of Finland. Swedes regularly go to their cottages on the thousands of small islands off their coast, just as Finns do, both by the sea and on the lakes. Swedes like their princess cakes, just like Finns. Swedes are mostly Lutheran, as are Finns.

But the two nations are different indeed. Swedes are perceived by Finns as a bit "snooty" and "arrogant". They are still believed to be inwardly thinking of their eastern neighbours as a kind of colony of their kingdom, which in fairness is probably not quite true now. Swedes are not part of the European Union and this enhances the opinion that they feel different from their Nordic partners such as Finland, Norway, and Denmark. Swedes are all blond (with a few exceptions, of course). Lots of their genes come from the Danish Vikings; after all, it was an easy hop across the water for the Danes to land on Swedish shores. Finns on the other hand are a mixture of Nordic and middle-European races that are represented respectively by slim tall blond individuals and short, stocky dark-haired people. Sweden never had to be concerned with the division between East and West, able to use Finland as its buffer, in its accepted isolation and neutrality, while Finland constantly had to debate whether to please the Russian giant on one side or the Western democracies on the other.

All the same, Finland and Sweden cannot stay apart. The short border that unites them in the north is not just a geographical link. Financially the ties between the two countries have become of increasing importance and some of the largest mergers or takeovers have taken place in the last decade between conglomerates on both sides of the Gulf of Bothnia. Most southern and western towns in Finland have street names and directions in both languages. The TV2 channel broadcasts many programs including news reports in Swedish, and I have to shamefully confess that we can follow the news in this language better than in Finnish, although neither Celia nor I speak Swedish.

So Finnish-Swedish relations are like a marriage of convenience, with no horse or carriage or confetti. They are accepted simply because they are there, with no love or hate, but just a subtle tone of disinterest. And at least no bad animals, polluted clouds or prostitutes are thought to come from Sweden.

The national sport in both countries is ice hockey, something that can be compared to football in most nations of continental Europe. Finland and Sweden have traditionally been arch-rivals since the sport was invented, and on the days when a final match takes place for victory or defeat in an international competition, both countries fall silent. The traffic stops, and almost all of the five million Finns and the nine million Swedes are glued to the television screens. For the Finns, a defeat in ice hockey can always be accepted as long as it does not come at the hand of the Swedes. And victory against their neighbour is the sweetest of results.

Berries

Berries are everywhere in Finland. Finns love their berries and the juices they make from them. At least, they say they love them.

We ourselves used to have a number of berry plants in the garden – black berries, red berries and white berries. Every year, come July, the plants used to swell with their colourful fruits, and friends would always remark on the quantities we could pick and on the amount of juice that Celia could make. As they say, "Yeah, right!"

We used to cover the bushes with netting so as to stop the myriads of birds from stripping the plants bare of their fruits and then leaving their colourful droppings on the wooden floors of our porches. We also maintained a kind of possessive instinct towards our own berries. We just did not want the birds to have them. They were ours. Not that we would need so many anyway. In fact, I remember probably only a couple of times when we actually picked them, getting bitten by mosquitos and generally getting bored by the messy job. We filled some plastic buckets and the berries were put away in freezer bags. Celia used some for puddings and cake decorations; the rest was thrown away the following year.

I am sure it is the same for everyone, but, as I mentioned earlier in the book, berry picking is the national occupation, together with having saunas, smoking fish, baking bread, and chatting in shops.

You invite friends to pick your berries. (We found that this is in fact the best way to have your berries picked without having to do the work yourself.) You let your friends have some of the berries they have collected in their plastic buckets. Usually, your friends already have large quantities of berries in their freezers, either from their own gardens or from other friends' gardens, and they will probably end up giving some of your berries away to some of their own friends, who again would have their freezers already full with the previous year's berries. And so it goes on.

Having berries in the freezer gives Finnish women a sense of security and the courage to face the oncoming winter with the knowledge that they can prepare juices for colds, tummy aches, headaches, fever, and other discomforts. Celia feels happy and secure if she has potatoes in the larder, although she has never made juice from them. Finnish women must have berries.

All the same, after stressing the importance and the pleasure of berry picking, many people we have encountered have quietly revealed that they hate the job. It is messy, sticky, boring, and hot from the July sun and at the height of the mosquito season, but like all uncomfortable traditions, it has to be maintained with a smile.

The berry bushes are long gone from our garden now. We let Juhani and Iris take two or three and gave the others to various friends. I have no idea what Juhani and Iris have done with our bushes, since they have moved into an apartment on the third floor of a building with two balconies. They were very happy to have the plants anyway. And our mosquitos have definitely diminished in number.

A couple of years ago we visited the parents of a good friend in their pleasant home on the outskirts of Turku, the old Finnish capital city. We were made very welcome by the elderly couple, who offered us coffee and cakes. The lady was a small neat woman with a strong personality and a warm smile. Her husband was a jovial kind man who at the age of eighty-two had his own computer room in the immaculately kept apartment.

We sat with them around the kitchen table, and we enjoyed their friendliness and spontaneity, despite it being our first encounter with them. Mamma (as the lady was called by her family when she became a grandmother) at one point opened the freezer and showed us the large quantity of berries in it. Our friends explained that, like all Finnish housewives, Mamma loved to have plenty of berries in the freezer. They made her feel safe. Some would be used for juices; the rest would probably stay in the freezer until next year when they might be thrown away to be followed by more recent pickings. Mamma reminded me of my grandmother.

I used to find our berry bushes untidy, ugly, and invasive, and I hated berry picking – even the very limited amount of berry picking I ever did. I hated my fingers becoming black and sticky. I hated the back ache that I suffered after spending some time bent over the bushes trying to get to the best berries that were always hidden under low branches. I hated everything connected with the job. Having said all this, I have to admit that I liked berries fresh from the bushes, when I would pick them and eat them as I walked past, or cooked and in cakes, or as a complement to black sausages or pork, or even in a nice salad on a summer's day.

In the little old wood that we acquired a few years ago by a small lake, most of the ground is covered in blueberries. They are small sturdy plants with strong minute leaves, shiny in their intense tone of green. Unfortunately on the few occasions when Celia decided to go and pick the blueberries, she found, much to her dismay, that bears had been there before us and must have had great blueberry parties. The large footprints left behind that had squashed the small plants to the ground were the proof that bears love blueberries. I hope their tongues became all blue in punishment for the theft.

Berry picking in Finland is as important as mushroom picking.

We know nothing about mushrooms and we cannot distinguish the edible from the poisonous ones. We like mushrooms, and Celia often cooks them in a variety of ways. A great many Finns have a deep knowledge of mushrooms and make regular expeditions to places that are generally kept secret, where they spend hours collecting them.

In fact, Finland is a great producer of mushrooms. The thick damp forests are ideal terrain for this strange product, and even the famous porcini – traditionally considered the exclusive discovery of Italy – grow in such abundance that they are actually exported to Italy and Italians even come to Finland especially to pick them, although being Italians they would never openly admit it.

I remember one warm summer day Juhani and Iris kindly suggested taking us mushroom picking on a small island on Paijanne, where they regularly went in secret so as not to disclose its rich mushroom fields to others.

It was a time when Juhani still had his motorboat, a small but comfortable boat with a cabin, a sitting area, and a couple of berths. Juhani's knowledge of Paijanne was undisputed after so many years of serious fishing for his business hours on end every night. We went east for about forty minutes until we reached a small calm bay and the anchor was dropped. We had to climb into the small rowing boat to go ashore, as the water became too shallow for the motorboat.

Luckily, the water by then was calm. Celia has never been fond of small boats, and on many occasions her nerves have got the better of her. For example, one time in Devon we spent a few days in a small town gloriously blessed by a beautiful estuary that opened up into the English Channel. We visited some friends on their magnificent polished-wood sailing boat that was moored in the middle of the estuary, and after a few drinks we were loaded into a small dinghy to be taken back to land. Celia became anxious about stepping down from the large boat into the small inflatable object floating by the side, and the result was that her behind went into the sea. She had to sit in a restaurant for dinner with wet jeans and underwear. And at the time she did not even drink alcohol, so that could not be the excuse.

Back to our small expedition. It looked as if the island had never seen a human creature before us. We felt we were in a different world. There was a strong musky smell from the damp vegetation and ground. Trees, rotted by centuries of temperamental weather, were just lying dead amidst rocks that had mysteriously dropped from somewhere. Our rubber boots sank into the wet peaty terrain. We expected some prehistoric monster to appear from behind every bush. The silence was eerie and the colours splendid.

We walked for about ten minutes to an opening in the vegetation, and suddenly we saw them: hundreds of mushrooms showing their heads everywhere. I have no idea what kind they were, and the name that Iris mentioned to us was immediately forgotten. She pointed at the ones that we could pick, and diligently we started our job, filling our buckets and regularly checking with Iris that we had not collected any dangerous ones. We spent over an hour filling our four buckets with no problem and chatting all the time, occasionally stopping and stretching our backs for a small rest. It was most enjoyable, and mostly because nobody else was there.

Back on the "big" boat, we had coffee and pirakka – an original Karelian home-baked pie – that Iris had prepared with rice and chopped eggs. It is one of the many Karelian traditional dishes. The pirakka tasted excellent.

When Juhani dropped us back home, Iris gave us a good quantity of the mushrooms we had picked. I cannot remember how Celia prepared them, but they were delicious.

Our friend Paula is another expert when it comes to mushrooms, and in autumn she always makes expeditions, often on her own despite the possibility of encounters with bears or wolves, to "her" private locations where mushrooms grow in large quantities. She has never revealed to us where she goes, even though she knows only too well that we would never pick mushrooms. Like everyone else who loves mushroom picking, she is very protective of her secret.

Yes, bears and wolves. A few years ago the environmentalists managed to convince the government to allow wolves to be put back in the wild of the Finnish countryside, releasing them from captivity so as to re-establish a balance (they claimed) in the forest population. They seem to have forgotten that though in the past wolves and men inhabited the forests and feared and respected each other, today's wolves, grown in captivity, have been close to people for decades and have even learnt that people feed them. They have no fear of people and no fear of coming to villages in search of food.

The result is that dogs, cats, and a variety of other domestic animals have disappeared and that wolves have been seen in small towns both at night and during the day. Children can no longer walk alone through wooded areas. People are no longer happy to walk alone in forests. I have to confess that I would not feel totally safe going mushroom picking or berry picking in isolated locations, in fear that I might encounter a pack of wolves.

Sometimes I wish that the city politicians knew a bit more about their country and would not just blame the Russians.

The Finns

They can look very serious and formal all the time. They like to have business discussions. They all want to be businessmen (or women). They walk through a door, completely ignoring the people behind them and allowing the door to slam in their faces. They push through a crowded place as if the world could come to an end any minute. They eat fast and quietly. They do not stand up when introduced to ladies, and they call everybody by first names (such an unpleasant American import). I am generalizing, of course, and there are exceptions, but not many.

But they are also friendly, honest, punctual, observant of all laws and regulations, funny, helpful, clean, respectful of authority, good drivers (generally, but here again there are many exceptions), nationalistic, politically incorrect (what a blessing!), and genuinely timid. They also love their free coffees and art.

I have deeply considered all of the above, and I do feel that each of my descriptions requires a thorough analysis and explanation so that my definitions are not misunderstood or taken out of context and found offensive – something that I do not intend them to be in the slightest.

I gave earlier the example of the gentleman sitting in his car, outside a supermarket while his wife was slogging across the road with a crate of beer and some carrier bags and had to load the car boot herself while the presumed husband simply sat and waited. This was certainly not an isolated case. In the old days, the man worked in the forest to get the meagre daily food and then returned home expecting his wife to have washed and cleaned his clothes and prepared his food after seeing to the children, to the animals, to the vegetable patch, to baking, to picking berries, to clearing the snow from the path, and to feeding the birds. These old ways still left a legacy in today's life.

I remember years ago when some friends took us to visit the museum in Verla. This museum is an old paper mill that UPM (one of the largest paper companies in the world) decided to close some fifty years before and convert into a showpiece of industrial life in post-war Finland. The place is regularly visited by both Finns and foreign tourists from many parts of the world, and some of the history of the mill and its labourers is shown on films projected in different languages at regular intervals in one of the old warehouses

When we sat in the large cold shed that had been a store room for the finished products, watching the black and white images on the screen mounted on the brick wall, we were quite staggered to see how the men who worked in the mill would go home after their shift, put a harness on their wives, attach them to a plough, and lead them through a field that needed seeding and working, albeit without whipping them. The women were the work-horses of the family. And that was only some sixty years ago, when the Marshall Plan was in full swing to rebuild Europe after the war and when the first TV sets had already started appearing in a number of countries.

It does not mean that Finland was backwards. It was simply that its deeply rooted hard-working attitudes in the forests had not changed as yet. People were still concerned with the simple task of having bread on the table, and they could not afford the niceties and pleasantries of etiquette. Both women and men had to work very hard and everything in life had to be grabbed whenever and however possible or it might be lost in someone else's hands.

Through the generations this feeling has remained to this day, and although global travel and the spread of good education is rapidly changing it, Finnish society is still a self-centred one, where consideration for others (unless guided by authority) is small and the most important thing is oneself. It is a heritage from life in the forest, where there was limited contact with fellow Finns, and from the predominant need to survive the harsh conditions and the particularly hazardous winters.

Years ago someone somewhere, in one of the small communities in the forests, told us a little anecdote that depicts the Finnish country spirit. If you had a stream coming through your land and found sawdust in it, you decided to go to war with whoever was living above you and had made his or her presence felt to you. The invader was a threat.

Some Finns more than others like to indulge in their difficult past, giving it a romantic colour and making it an object of pride and a distinguishing difference from the rest of the world. To the uninitiated they may appear to dwell excessively on their past poverty and struggle to the point of boredom. The truth is that less than a hundred years of history as a nation is an incredibly short time to forget a difficult life that had existed for centuries, especially for a society grown in its own isolation and fear – fear of the West and of the East, but also fear of hunger. The fact is also that climatic conditions in Finland can actually be so terrible and extreme that people's own individual home becomes the only acceptable and understandable world for them. Nothing else counts. This is something that the passing visitor or the family searching for Father Christmas in Lapland and enjoying the one-off showpiece sauna and the hole in the ice, set up for the tourist business may never fully appreciate.

For some six months a year the ground freezes and becomes a layer of solid concrete covered in deep snow where nothing can grow. The lakes become immense ice blocks where fishing is impossible – well, almost impossible, except for drilling holes in the ice.

Talking of drilling holes in the ice, we did it ourselves on a few occasions using a drill that Celia gave me for one of my birthdays. It was hard work to make the hole through the thick ice and the wonderful splashing noise made by the drill when it actually reached the water was rewarding and fulfilling. When the sharp tip of the drill finally gets through the whole layer of ice, sometime eighty or ninety centimetres thick, the water constricted under the surface happily finds its way out and gushes up for a few seconds with a satisfying sound.

We sat on folding cloth chairs in the freezing sun with our short fishing rods, doing exactly as friends had told us: moving the line at regular intervals, clearing it from ice, making sure that it reached almost the bottom of the lake, where apparently the fish goes to find warmer waters. We caught nothing, despite copying other people we had watched from our windows. We had seen them change places every now and then, and we had visions of the lake becoming like a colander and crashing because of the number of holes that perforated the surface after a horde of enthusiasts had spent a few hours constantly searching for new places to drill.

Perhaps the fish did not understand our language, or perhaps every fish was frozen stiff on the bottom of the lake and had no energy to swim towards the colourful maggots that we had bought. We caught nothing.

I asked a friend once what would happen if, by a stroke of good luck, someone caught a fish that was too fat for the hole and could not be pulled through. The immediate reply – given with a straight and inscrutable face – was, "You just have to wait for spring when the ice melts." And people think the Finns have no sense of humour!

Back to the winter harshness, most birds migrate south and other animals hibernate. The old wooden forest cottages turn into refrigerators with frosty windows, in which families can survive only around the huge fireplaces that are constantly burning wood. Shopping of any kind becomes an adventure, as the stony and uneven forest tracks become skiing paths. The old hand-operated water pumps in the gardens stop working as they get blocked by ice. In these cottages people lived and grew old, their faces lined by the fight with the temperament and cruelty of the weather.

No wonder the Finns look stern. There is nothing much to laugh about in the picture I have painted, and it is no wonder that most Finnish films still show the torment of the soldiers during the Winter Wars and the tribulations of forest inhabitants trying to survive their life-long struggle.

The positive element that emerges from all this and that does make the Finns rather unique in the general context of today's nations is the sense of unity and pride. All Finns feel very much Finnish and are proud to be Finnish. The respect for their Flag and for their national institutions is admirable. Many a house (including ours after we had one fixed in the highest point of our small plot) has a flag pole in the garden, and on the days marked in the calendars as Flag Days (special celebrations, festivities, historical dates, etc.) each flag pole flies with pride the white and blue national flag. And we do the same (in addition to flying the Union Jack on some special occasions and on birthdays and family reunions). We like to do this, and the flag looks lovely flapping in the wind.

What Lonroth and Snellman did when they managed to give birth to the national language was certainly helped by the existing feeling of unity that the communities already had but did not know how to express in a coordinated manner. Every Finn has a neighbour, and every neighbour is a Finn. We have been used to consider our neighbours as the people living in the apartment next door or in the house along the road or opposite. In Finland everyone who lives within the administrative boundary of a community that may extend for several kilometres in all directions from the central town or village is considered a neighbour. And neighbours are generally there to help, to comfort, to gossip with, to have saunas with, and to fish with. The original hunter-gatherer groups have only really changed in size but not in spirit.

One of the most amusing aspects of the Finnish psychology is the phrase that I have heard so many times from people who are not in mainstream employment: "I am a businessman." The strange concept of business, which seems to be so important in village communities, is that buying and selling – whether on a market stall or at a country fair – makes almost everyone a businessman or businesswoman. As such, business people do not have meetings, but they do have discussions, and they expect interested parties to make them offers for what they want to buy, rather than being told the price. "Okay then, make me an offer." That is how things are normally sold and purchased. So you fall into the trap, make an offer that the seller considers too low, and that is the end of the deal! No room for negotiation or re-thinking. Loppu! That is the end of it! It is an interesting way of doing business.

I have had myself a few direct experiences of this. The first time was when I mentioned to Juhani our interest in purchasing the house that we had been renting for some eight years. Always keen to make money, Juhani's answer was very quick. "Okay, make me an offer." It seemed a strange approach, one that I had never encountered before during my many years in business and marketing, and quite simply I had no idea where to start. What would be the reasonable market value of the house? What could I offer? It had to be an amount low enough to be attractive to me and high enough to be interesting to Juhani.

I decided to contact my bank and explain the dilemma. The manager of the local branch met me one day, together with one of the Bank's real estate experts, to try and establish the current value of the property. They examined it inside and outside. They had a look at the garden and at the lake shoreline. They discussed between themselves. (Well, I would not have understood their Finnish discussion anyway.) After a while they proceeded to stand back to back in the middle of the drive and each wrote on a separate card the estimate that each of them had reached without any conferring. They showed me the two figures (that were almost identical) and finally suggested that the offer to be put forward to Juhani should be based on that, with a ten per cent flexible margin on either side.

Although it seemed to me a rather unusual way to go about things, I accepted that everything had been done correctly and I prepared a written offer that, in addition to a price, also explained how I had come to it and pointed out some of what, in my opinion, were slight shortcomings of the building, mostly due to its twenty-something years of life, beaten by sun, wind, and snow. In England a surveyor would have been called in and a full report expected, even before a possible purchase would be considered.

Needless to say, Juhani refused the offer point black and took umbrage at some of the comments I had made, especially about some visible signs of dampness in the corner of the shower room, about the state of the roof, about the fact the shoreline apparently did not belong to the property, and so on. That was the end of it. There was no room for further discussions or negotiations. My sensible offer, made in the absence of a selling price, was discarded. In fact, I never actually had a formal reply from Juhani but was simply advised by his daughter-in-law (our neighbour) that the offer had been rejected. Juhani did not speak to me for a few months after the episode. Finns can be very proud.

It was almost over one year later that Juhani suddenly had second thoughts about the whole matter and contacted me again, this time asking me if we were still interested in purchasing the house. He produced a price at which he would be prepared to sell. This was a rather different approach and one that was more familiar to me. The whole transaction took a different colour and a much more "business-like" tone, and in the end an agreement was reached after a meeting at Juhani's and Iris' lakeside Summer cottage, during which Iris left the room, since she was unbelievably concerned that Juhani and I would have a punch-up. It is a fact that Finns are not prepared for direct confrontations of ideas and would rather walk away and grumble behind the scenes than openly express their opinion or argue their reasons, in fear that the counterpart might never speak to them again.

When Iris realized that in fact the sounds she could hear coming from the sitting room were laughter, because of the occasional humour that I was putting into the conversation for the purpose of taking the sharp edges away, she came back relieved and offered us some drinks and cakes.

It was an experience. And it was an experience to see how houses are bought and sold in Finland. What you see is what you get. There is no point in raising doubts about the state of repair or inspecting the building in detail. That is what is for sale. Take it or leave it. If the condition of the place is not satisfactory, you ought to look for something else. Full stop. Someone will always be prepared to buy it as it is. On the other hand, once the seller and the buyer have agreed on the transaction, everything is straightforward. There are no solicitors to delay the process and no estate agents to complicate matters. It is a deal between the two interested parties and nobody else, and it may be concluded in a matter of days once the sale and purchase document has been verified and signed by an acting notary. It is an example of the absence of bureaucracy and of the straight character of the Finns.

Things may be not be so straight when Finns drive.

Finland has produced some of the best drivers in the world – a great achievement, if we stop and think of the small population of this country. I am not just referring to the three F1 world champions, but to the great many rally champions who have become household names among motor racing fans around the globe. I think it is fair to say that in relation to the country's population, Finland is ahead of Britain, Italy, and France when it comes to F1 world champions and rally champions. The nature of the forest roads and their difficult conditions both in Summer and in Winter offer a good training ground to the Finns right from a young age, and the obligatory studded tyres that have to be fitted during the long months of snow and ice allow them to acquire extreme and almost natural control in situations that are extraordinary for many non-Finns.

All country roads are a challenge for drivers, in summer because they are covered with loose gravel laid in preparation for the winter snow and ice, and in the winter months simply because of the snow on the ground.

I still remember the shock of driving on one such road, the first time we ventured out of our village and decided to see some of the surrounding countryside. It was late summer, and the road had been covered with a layer of gravel, large loose chippings waiting to be sunk into the ground about three months later when autumn would quickly turn into winter. Once off the tarmac of a main road, I found myself driving on a moving bed of small rocks that made steering precarious and bends hazardous. To crown it all, the road was like a helter-skelter following the hilly nature of the ground. Like most country roads, as we have learnt, it had simply been laid by removing the trees that were in the way, and it did not cut into hills or humps but just followed the uneven surface. Occasionally the humps were so steep that I could not see what was waiting for me on the other side – generally, a sharp bend. It was a lesson in driving such as I had never had before, but at least the road was empty.

That is the point. Outside major cities, roads are empty. One can drive for tens of kilometres without encountering another vehicle in either direction, so concentration goes easily out of the window, and the mind wanders to searching for elks or bears among the thick rocky woods, to past memories of holidays with the children, to what is likely to be on the dinner table that evening, to friends, and so on. There are no gear changes needed, few bends that require attention, no traffic lights, and no other cars to look out for. And that is when interesting things may happen, like falling asleep at the wheel or suddenly being confronted by an elk crossing the road. Its lanky legs look almost disjointed as it walks unevenly and obliviously out of the wood, ignoring the unaware driver who may happen to be on the road just at that time. In Finland the tragic accidents caused by these almost blind animals when they decide to go from one wood to another across the road are one of the major causes of death. On a few occasions we have ourselves seen these majestic-looking animals quietly climb the roadside and cross the road silently, sometimes followed by their little ones, and we have had to slow down to avoid the impact. Luckily, we have always seen them early and at a reasonable distance, but often at dusk when they search for water pools, the danger can be serious and fatal.

Off the road and in the forests, elks are placid animals that go about their business of eating grass and ruining trees by eating the bark, keeping themselves away from humans. They have a great ability to camouflage themselves among trees and bushes, and they are difficult to spot. We have seen a few, perhaps half a dozen, in all the time we have spent in Finland; a couple with babies staring at us from behind a trunk, curious and suspicious.

Their number has been growing to an unreasonable level over the years, and the Government has been adopting a careful policy of culling them, officially allocating quota to selected individuals who in October or November patrol the forests wearing the almost compulsory red caps (so as to be easily recognized by others and avoid being shot by mistake). This intelligent policy is working well, and at least for some years to come the trees and the forests will be preserved and drivers will be a little safer.

Having no traffic to contend with, drivers relax and sit back, activate the cruise control, and let the cars do the rest. Until they reach a roundabout, that is. Yes, roundabouts. Still a rather peculiar novelty here, having been introduced during the last ten years, roundabouts even today represent one of the major areas of failure when it comes to Finns taking appropriate action and letting other road users know their intentions. The fact that what used to be a straightforward crossroads intersection between major roads is suddenly now a roundabout is confusing. A good example is the one on the approach to Jamsa where the road cuts across the Tampere/Jyvaskyla road, with all the consequences of accidents that occasionally occurred because drivers did not stop in time after cruising downhill towards Jamsa as they approached from the south.

A friend of ours, who owned a nearby hotel, after a visit to England where he marvelled at roundabouts, pressed the local council to create one at such the crossroad so as to reduce the number of fatalities and hopefully stop wounded people from rushing into his hotel suffering from shock or injuries. He succeeded, and a roundabout appeared, nicely designed, with a tall stone monument in the middle representing a huge roll of paper in recognition of the major source of funds in the area thanks to a couple of major paper mills. But that is when the fun began. Puzzled drivers found themselves lost as to where to go and how. Certainly not straight over, but what about going round it? Indicators? If so which one? Right or left?

We have learnt that the best thing to do as you approach a roundabout is to stop and move on only when no other cars are around. You never know where drivers are going, and generally making assumptions about what direction they will be taking in the absence of any indication can be disastrous. We have seen drivers go all the way round and end up facing the direction they came from without the slightest hint of the use of indicators. We have seen drivers needing to turn right and using the left indicator and vice versa. We have seen drivers turning right or left and stopping halfway through, only to then change their minds and go straight ahead with no indicators flashing.

Jamsa is now full of roundabouts, and with the limited amount of traffic that circulates in a small country town, they should be the optimal solution to congestion and accidents. It may be so one day. For the time being, they could be the cause of many more disasters were it not for the fact that everyone approaches a roundabout with extreme caution and, thankfully, at no speed.

It is a little like car parks. After a long drive on a deserted road, coming from a quiet empty village where the only hazard is represented by old people suddenly cutting in front of you and then proceeding to drive at a tortoise pace oblivious of anything around them, the Finnish driver arrives at his destination and has to park his car among other cars. If more than one car is moving in the same car park, confusion takes place. Everyone stops, not knowing what the other driver will do or where he or she will go. Long moments of hesitation and fear follow. We just find it amusing and refreshing; there is nothing one can do but wait patiently. After all, what are a few minutes in a lifetime? We have been corrupted by years of traffic and rush in large cities – London, Milan, New York, and Paris – where everyone is crazy. After many years in Finland we are beginning to learn. And in any case Finnish drivers are either exceptionally good or very doubtful and slow. There is no in between.

We also found that you can easily get lost in the Finnish countryside.

August is rally time in central Finland. It used to be called the Rally of the Thousand Lakes, and it used to come around our village in the last week of August. Now it is called the Neste Rally (from the sponsorship of a major oil company) – and arrives earlier in August. On rally weekends our village changes from a quiet soporific place of some 3,000 souls into a busy and noisy parking lot for rally followers and their motorbikes, camper vans and trailers. They always leave behind an incredible amount of rubbish and beer cans.

We went to one of the rally sessions with Tuomo, many years ago, and we experienced the noise and excitement of the colourful cars thumping the ground as they approached our viewing point, noisily because of their lack of silencers. It must be the only motor racing event in the world at which spectators can actually walk along the racing track of country lanes and just move out of the way at the last moment, when cars approach, warned by a single whistle from the stewards. It borders on complete madness.

The racers came and went in seconds at a ridiculously crazy speed, announcing their approach by making the ground shudder and then disappearing behind a cloud of dust and pebbles. One after the other they flew by, some faster than others. We do not intend to do it again. I found it uncomfortable, dusty, and dangerous. The best viewing points are normally by bends, exactly where the cars are likely to spin off and crash into you. Like the bulls, freely rushing

95

through Pamplona, the risk and the fight with death are probably the very elements that attract the fans.

One year we decided to go out for a drive on a rally weekend. This was a very bad decision. We could hear the helicopters flying overhead, keeping an eye on the racing tracks and on the spectators, and we made sure we avoided turning down one of the many small roads leading to the start or the finish of the session. We had a nice drive through the country and saw new places, all with their small wooden cottages and saunas, all immersed in beautiful woods, rich and lush after the months of summer.

On the way back I decided to take a minor road, knowing exactly the direction to take, when we suddenly started noticing people of all ages sitting outside their houses or leaning on their garden gates, chatting, drinking, and relaxing, as if waiting for something to come by. They certainly were not waiting for us. We felt it must be something to do with the rally and not with two elderly English people out for a leisurely Saturday drive, so we did not wave to them as we passed their front gates.

Suddenly the road became a narrow track with people walking all in the same direction, and we were soon stopped by a young man wearing the typical yellow fluorescent vest that gives an air of authority to people who normally do not have any authority. He asked us to park at the end of a long line of cars by the side of the road, the left wheels precariously close to the edge and to the ditch. There was no way we could go any further. Two more young lads wearing the same yellow sleeveless tops that made them important "stewards" told us in broken English and with a lot of spitting on the ground that the start of the race was just at the end of the road and we could not move until all the racing cars had gone past to reach the starting line. No pleading would convince them to let us even go back. Celia had planned an early dinner, and all we wanted was to go home.

Other cars kept arriving after us, and the line of parked vehicles behind ours became so long that more and more we were getting blocked in with no hope of being released. We had several semi-conversations with one of the two lads who seemed to be "in charge" and who had the privilege of a two-band radio in his hand, but we were told unequivocally that the racing cars were now beginning to arrive and we could not be driving on that road until they had all reached the start. We resigned ourselves, knowing that what should have been a short pleasant drive had now become a long and tiring afternoon, especially as we were not interested in the rally.

Four or five racing cars in all imaginable colours and sponsorship liveries went by at slow speed, making terrific noises through their lack of silencers. The drivers did not even acknowledge our presence, something that we found somewhat offensive since we seemed to have been high-jacked by their sport. Suddenly and with no explanation whatsoever, after a few exchanges on his radio, the "head steward" told us that he would help us turn the car round in the narrow road and we could drive back, on condition that we went very slowly with the hazard lights flashing and right by the edge of the road, since the competitors were still arriving along the same road from the opposite direction.

It was not easy to turn our little Nissan in the very limited space available, but the two lads – who apparently had radioed somewhere that an elderly couple from England was going to be moving on the road at the same time as the racing cars would be arriving from the opposite direction – were helpful, and after a few more spits in between phrases in English, they waved us off. I drove as close as possible to the side of the road and as slowly as possible with the hazard lights flashing as instructed, but when two or three racing cars confronted us even at their low speed, I have to admit that I did not feel very comfortable, and the thought of getting in the way of a rally world champion on his way to a race made me feel even less comfortable. I was very pleased when we reached the turning that I had missed in the first place and we took the right road home.

I am sure that some of the racing papers the following day must have reported about the old English couple in a small grey Nissan who almost found themselves competing against the likes of Tommi Makinen and Colin McRae in the local session of the Neste Rally!

· · · · · ·

It was soon after meeting Aulikki several years ago at her Summer painting exhibition that she held for the first time in her lovely old farmhouse in the forest, that we were asked to join her and her husband, as well as a number of their friends, for a late Christmas evening of singing. Somehow we got on well with Aulikki right from the moment we saw her stepping out of her house on a lovely warm August afternoon. We were strolling in her garden, admiring her paintings that were scattered among the old wooden outbuildings, amidst other people who had come from almost everywhere. We introduced ourselves, and she marvelled at the fact that some people from England were visiting her small exhibition. Her English was good, full of perfect and formal expressions that are not so colloquial but are typical of a well-educated person who likes to be perfect at what she does. She was tall, with short blond hair, and bare-footed. After living in the United States, Brazil, Switzerland, and Africa, she had the air of a British colonial wife of a Colonel, with the usual sense of insecurity and self-assurance mixed together, that made her pleasant and interesting. We became friends, and we still consider her and her husband among our closest Finnish friends.

When we received the invitation to the singing evening, we did not know what to expect. Christmas had gone over a week earlier, but we were told that we would be singing some Christmas carols as well. We knew that Finns love singing in groups. We knew that Finns love singing at ceremonies, at funerals, at weddings, and at dinner celebrations. We had been in restaurants where the owner would suddenly start singing lovely old traditional tunes without a hint of embarrassment or shyness. We knew singing is a way for Finns to feel togetherness and unity.

We arrived at Aulikki's place, after a hair-raising drive on a helter-skelter country road, on which, if you were not careful, you risked getting stuck between steep hills and dips. Many cars were already parked by the sides of the road in the freezing night. The house was warm and welcoming and after the usual introduction and a walk around the large tupa where people were sitting on the long wooden benches, worn out and polished by centuries of human behinds that had rested on it, we were handed the sheets with the selection of tunes that Aulikki had made.

With the help of her brother-in-law's guitar we started singing some of the tunes. We recognized a number of them that were famous and familiar Christmas carols. Some were old folk songs, usually about hardship and tiring forest work. Others reflected on wars, when the cruelty of fighting had taken loved ones away. Some were happy motifs, reminiscing about children's simple games played outside, bare-footed and joyful, while cakes and rye bread were baked in the huge log fire of the tupa. Most were unknown to us, but even the famous carols seemed different in Finnish. In fact, we tried our best to read the printed words on the sheets and follow the music, only to find that in most cases everyone had moved on to a new line while we were still struggling to go through the immense number of vowels and consonants of single words, with the result that we were always left behind. It was fun, and we had a great evening. Finns love their singing.

We have been invited back many times by Aulikki, and her singing evenings have become a yearly event, attended by people who come from as far as Helsinki. The single guitar of her brother-in-law has been joined by another musician. The song sheet has become thicker and more professional. The Finnish words have not changed much for us, and we still struggle to keep pace with the others, but we always have a great time, and somehow we feel that after many years we now fully belong to Finland and understand the spirit of the singing. It is one more important way for these people to feel united.

· · · · · ·

Dancing and singing are two major occupations for the Finns.

Singing and reciting verses provide a way to be connected with the past and with the others around you. I remember one summer's day years ago when we joined a group of locals for a day coach trip around central Finland. Most of us were elderly. (Yes, I have to admit that I consider myself and Celia elderly now.) Some we knew, while others were new faces. Everyone was friendly and jovial, despite having the usual stern faces to start with. I have no idea who organized the trip. For us it was a day out and an opportunity to see places where we had not been as yet.

The coach driver seemed to follow a certain logic and we stopped first at a kind of open-air art exhibition at the house of a local artist. The place was lovely and the grounds stunning. The art pieces – wooden bears and eagles scattered among plants and flowers – were not, but we had coffee and cakes and the opportunity to get to know our fellow travellers.

After another stop at an old leather and shoe factory, we visited Kallela's home and studio, like a pilgrimage to one of the most important figures in early ^{twentieth}-century Finnish art. The house was stunning and imposing, with its round wooden columns and its alcoves and crevices, and it enjoyed the most beautiful view of the lake below. It also had gloomy and mysterious tones, reflected in some of the large paintings by the famous artist who came from Sweden and changed his name from Gallen to Kallela. Some of his works on the walls were scenes from the Kalevala, with frightening characters and images of war and death, and some were clearly influenced by his Masonic interests, full of symbolism and mystery. All this was explained to us by his granddaughter and his great grandson who very kindly took time to tell us about their famous ancestor's life.

After that we stopped briefly by Runeberg's Fountain. Runeberg is the most revered poet in modern Finnish literature. His statue stands at the very centre of Helsinki's Esplanade, and calendars show a "Runeberg Day" when the national flag should be flown. The "fountain" is really only a little pond fuelled by a natural underground stream in a not-too-interesting location, but it is a kind of national symbol. The fact the Mr Runeberg stood by the pool and wrote some of his lyrics or simply sat around it in contemplation makes it special to the Finns. So there we were, all of twenty of us, standing around the murky waters of the pool, when someone produced a little pocket-size book of Runeberg's works and started reading some of the verses. It was surreal and moving at the same time – some twenty elderly and middle-aged people standing by a small pool in a rather dark opening in the wood, listening in silence to Runeberg's rhymes being read in homage to the great poet.

On the way back a few popular tunes were sung on the coach, and a little speech was given by the lady who apparently had organized the trip, thanking the driver for taking us around safely. Everyone applauded the speech and the driver, and a little token was given to him as a gesture of appreciation. The community spirit was there, and we felt part of the small congregation.

We used to regularly watch a program on one of the TV channels that broadcast singing summer evenings from Tampere. It came from a small park by the old Finlayson brick buildings. The audience was made up of a great variety of people – families with children, visitors, and local residents. They occasionally wore those see-through plastic raincoats that had been given to them by the organizers to protect them from the occasional rain, the ones that make everyone everywhere look a bit ridiculous but that are practical if the dry weather suddenly changes its mind.

The singer on stage was always a popular figure, happy and entertaining, and he never had any problem in getting the whole of the audience swinging in their seats and singing in unison.

The television screen always showed the text of the songs line by line, and we ourselves tried many times to join in the singing from our armchairs, more often than not failing to read the longest (and not just the longest) words and falling further and further behind the rest of the audience. It was fun. Everyone seemed to enjoy themselves, and the singing appeared to bring everyone together in the Tampere Park whether it rained or the sun was shining. They all felt Finnish.

Dancing is something else that young and old love to practice almost everywhere. Driving across the Finnish countryside, especially on a Friday evening, it is not uncommon to suddenly see cars parked in a field by a wooden barn hidden among the trees. The old and often rather dilapidated building is alive with people dancing to the music from a local band of basic instruments. Couples dance in the "old style", where males lead females by holding them at the waist with one arm stretched, the hand holding the lady's hand. There is none of the modern fancy rock or rap dancing, just tango, one-step, slow waltz, quick-step, and so on.

The places are always full, and couples squeeze among one another, some in time with the music and many completely out of rhythm, but it does not matter. Everyone is dancing and feeling part of a small community of Finns.

Celia has always hated that kind of traditional dancing. I have always loved it. I started dancing by instinct, holding my first partner when I was around fifteen. It happened one summer in a small village on the hills of Tuscany, when the parents of the school friend I was spending a holiday with decided to have some of their own friends over to their old farmhouse for an evening of eating, drinking, and dancing. The friends brought their sons and daughters too, and I found myself overcoming my nerves and asking a pretty girl called Berta to dance to the sound of the tune of "Scandal in the Sun", so popular and catching in the early sixties. I am sure my steps were out of the ordinary and completely imaginative, but Berta and I seemed to move well together and in time with the music. I enjoyed it. I have no idea what happened to Berta after that summer. I just remember that she was the daughter of the local bank manager.

When Celia came into my life, I managed to have her around a dance floor a few times despite her two left feet, and I even declared my love to her while holding her to me, dancing to the famous (at the time) tune of "The Lion Sleeps Tonight", a song with wild African intonations. I think that was also the last time that Celia and I ever danced, maybe due to the shock that Celia experienced at my declaration of love.

Not long ago we visited Tampere with Eino and Pirkko, and after a lunch of sausages and sauerkraut we decided to have a coffee in a small place that looked at the same time hippy and bohemian. It was a nondescript place with a coffee-cum-bar at one end and a few tables in between a large variety of small plants that stood on the floor and on shelves. Some of the plants bore a great resemblance to the ones that are "popular" and very much enjoyed by hippy communities around the world, but maybe they were simply decorative and innocent. Music was playing in the background. A young couple who looked as if they had just come out of a Californian "Make Love Not War" leaflet were eating a plate of pasta at a nearby table, the pretty blond girl often glancing with a smile at our table, where unexpectedly ordinary people were having a coffee and a laugh.

Suddenly Eino got up, extended his hand to Pirkko, and invited her to dance. They moved on the small floor among the tables for a few minutes, to the young couple's – and our –amusement and then came back to finish their coffee with us, as if it had been the most natural thing in the world.

Finns love their dancing.

• • • • • •

I have hardly seen a race that eats as fast as the Finns. Our lunch and dinner times never seem to coincide with their times, and our food never seems to adapt to theirs.

We have seen Finns eat in different places, from a roadside hamburger place attached to a service station to a pleasant restaurant in the centre of a provincial town. No matter what they order or select, food is something to be ingested as quickly as possible, as a necessity. Eating does not seem an enjoyable occupation as it may be in countries like Greece, Italy, France or Spain. (Britain will soon join that league, after the determined efforts of a variety of so-called chefs who have tried repeatedly to convert a fish-and chip and mushy-pea-and-sausage society into a food-enjoying one).

How can you possibly "make" people enjoy food if the desire and the taste are not part of their life? Food is the result and the product of traditions, habits, troubles, and happiness, of winds and sun and moon and feasts and tragedies and religions and family ways and historical events and world catastrophes. Food is not simply a way of feeding your body. It is a way of enjoying life, not a mechanical or digital body-feeding clock.

In the fashionable haunts of Helsinki, society looks the same as anywhere else in the world's cities, enjoying the pleasures of good wine and well-prepared dishes, be these snails at Sgtringberg, a fish platter in the fish market, or a very small portion of whatever is ordered at Sipuli, overlooked by the imposing Orthodox Church. Champagne is the popular drink, and beautiful people are all around. The Hotel Kamp restaurant is always busy, as are most of the restaurants in the city, from the excellent Juri to Chez Dominique to the modern Grillit to Olu. We have been to innumerable good restaurants in Helsinki and in some of the towns along the south coast, and we have tasted superior food of different kinds, surrounded by Finns enjoying their Lucullan meals. Thanks to friends we have been introduced to many restaurants on our visits to Helsinki, some with an international colour, many with a strictly Finnish flavour. Some are very exotic, like the dark and over-furnished Shashlik that offers a warm and noisy Russian atmosphere, with a pretty singer and a balalaika player.

But Helsinki is Helsinki, an international city that, like all international cities, caters for visitors as well as for its own inhabitants. Outside Helsinki and Tampere and Turku and Porvoo food is usually just something on the plate, and Finns eat it, seemingly forgetting what their grandmothers cooked in a not-too-distant past and the pleasures of a Kalakukko (a terribly fattening and greasy but delicious pot of fish and bread) or a Laski Sosi (a pure injection of cholesterol, but a sheer enjoyment for the palate) or a Voileipa Kakku (a wonderful-tasting cake of bread and butter covered in savoury cream), all served in an old kitchen by the huge soapstone baking oven.

In the smaller towns or villages, where the real people are and where small communities maintain the true traditions of Finnish forest life, food is still a need, not a pleasure. Finns sit at a table and eat. I mean they hardly chew what they get into their mouths as fast as possible, as if the world were to end tomorrow. They do not often taste; they swallow and digest (and maybe sometimes they do not digest). Then they walk away, feeling that they have had their daily ration of fuel.

The natural necessity to satisfy their bodies has not changed from the times when in the forests they needed to satisfy their hunger by filling their stomach with whatever was available, knowing that the next man was always close to take the food away or that food might not be available tomorrow.

However, a food culture is now beginning. Finland has produced a number of very creative and capable chefs who in a great many television programs have started showing that food is not just the cold and technical act of eating and that old traditions and methods have their pride and qualities, as long as they are accepted and understood.

Some enthusiasts have even managed to establish, at times buried in forests, small restaurants in traditional old farmhouses that offer old-fashioned and neglected dishes, trying to revive the cooking of the ancestors. They are rare, but some have been successful and we are lucky to have one such place not too far away from us by the skiing slopes of Himos, one of the best-known skiing resorts in Finland. The Tila at Pata Pirtti is run by Tarja, a vivacious lady who has based her menu on local produce with the interest and love of a real culinary expert. We are regular visitors, and we have enjoyed many a meal of elk, reindeer, fish, or soup prepared from old granny recipes. Tila has existed for a few years now, and I am glad to see that more and more Finns are slowly appreciating the quality of its cuisine and ambience, as well as its local meat, berries, and wine.

Nowadays most Finns have a quick eleven o'clock lunch of a bun and a coffee or, if they feel adventurous, a kirsch and a coffee, and off they go until dinner, which for most consists of a few biscuits and cheese or a soup, potatoes, and bread. Later they may have the curved fat sausage, cooked over the hot stove while drinking beer in their sauna.

We know of friends who rarely appear to have anything else but bread and soup or salads and potatoes for dinner and maybe for the following day's lunch, despite the fact that they could certainly enjoy many more things. We ourselves have enjoyed such meals, leaving the table feeling adequately filled. This was precisely the purpose of food in the forests' past harsh conditions and poverty. It was always essential to fill the stomach and make sure the food lasted a few days. I am just wondering (and I am no dietician) whether the great numbers of people who are apparently suffering with heart problems in Finland are the result of this traditional and limited diet, which is no doubt the heritage of the times when food was hard to find in the forests and when in winter it was impossible to either buy it or grow it under the blanket of snow. Traditional soups were prepared to last a week, and stodgy filling food was served to give calories to bodies exposed to the extremes of the weather. Some of the traditional dishes that we have tried, thanks mostly to the efforts by Pirkko and Eino in making sure that we had a real taste of Finland, were truly great, but they all reflected the old need for the forest communities to fill their stomachs cheaply and quickly so as to go through another day of hard unforgiving work, rather than to give pleasure and appreciation for taste and quality. Fish, bread, and potatoes were certainly the main diet.

And Finnish potatoes are always something to write to your parents about. They seem to have a taste and a consistency that in most other potatoes appears to have gone with the wind. It maybe that Celia's cooking ability has something to do with it, but Finnish potatoes are special, whether they are mashed, roasted, cooked in garlic and herbs, or boiled. They are heaven! We have even learnt how to peel them at the table, using a fork and knife, holding them up like when you peel an orange. We were told that this is an important test of Finnishness. Children are taught to do it at a young age, and until they can master the job properly they are not considered grownups. For Finns, peeling potatoes is almost a kind of gentile bar mitzvah.

Potatoes are wonderful, but so is the fish. I never used to eat fish. Right from my childhood, fish was never a "proper" food for me. I found it tasteless, full of bones, and boring. I started eating fish in Finland from the time when Juhani and Iris took us to their island on Paijanne and smoked some white fish on an open fire over some large stones which made an impromptu barbeque. We thoroughly enjoyed this, sitting at a rough wooden table made out of two tree trunk halves. The fish was served simply with potatoes (back to the Finnish potato pleasure) and some herbs, and it had small bones that could be eaten with no problem. It tasted of the lake, of the clean air, of koivu. Delicious!

Ever since then, I have enjoyed fish. I have had it boiled in a pot on a stone fire by the shore of an island. I have had it with cream and dill and potatoes. (Again, these wonderful potatoes are everywhere.) I have had it smoked. We are lucky, of course, having as a neighbour a professional fisherman. Every night Jorma sails off into Paijanne with his two large boats, armed with radar and sonar and whatever else is needed to find the shoals. He works impossible hours until the early morning to make sure that his fish is delivered to supermarkets and outlets before the start of business. Some nights, looking out of our windows on Paijanne before going to bed, we see the lights of Jorma's boats appear from round the island opposite our house and aim for the boat shed. They gleam in the dark, almost like floating Christmas trees with their lights on. The fish is unloaded, separated by type, descaled, and gutted by machine; then it is placed into polystyrene containers and into cold storage, ready for the morning deliveries. Occasionally we buy fish straight from the boat shed, often from the small stall that Jorma's wife and daughters keep in the village during the summer months. It is always superbly fresh.

Jorma always fishes even in winter. First he breaks the ice on the lake, ensuring that right up until the thickness of the ice makes it impossible, his boats can cut through the freezing water and get to deeper pockets where the fish hide for warmth. Later he places nets through holes in the frozen surface and regularly checks his catch. He always makes a square hole in the ice, not too far from his boat shed, and covers it with a wooden board. It is like the hole I would make at the beginning of the freezing season, close to our shore, for me to dip into after my saunas. When the ice becomes too thick, I cannot break the layer, and that is when I can only hope that the snow is deep enough for me to roll in it without scratching some precious parts.

Jorma's ice hole is like a permanent fridge and is always kept liquid. Inside a round deep net holds the freshly caught fish – salmon, pike, white fish, bream, and the occasional trout – all swimming very happily in the freezing water until Jorma selects a fish for a customer. Then it is a matter of a quick knock on the head, a cut through the belly to remove the interiors, and a scrape with the knife to descale it, leaving the remainders on the frozen lake surface. Magpies, jays, and other scavengers will clean it up.

Once in autumn we were given some crayfish by a friend. It was still grey and almost translucent, freshly caught in a net. They were crawly little things, unpleasant to handle for the amateur, but they soon went into a pot of boiling water and acquired the usual red colour that we see in supermarkets. They were delightful and enjoyable, so we thought of buying a do-it-yourself net to lower into Paijanne by our jetty, hoping that we could get some crayfish meals out of it. We had been told by friends that it was easy and the method never failed.

The building of the net was an enterprise in its own right. The two large kidney-shaped sections would not stay together, and I felt that I needed four pairs of hands to keep all the pieces in place. After some two hours and a number of scratches to my hands and arms (and some colourful language) because of the sharpness of the zinc mesh, the cage was standing up on its own and it looked good. Attaching a piece of rope to the handle, I lowered it into the water of Paijanne, right by the side of the jetty where "expert" friends had told us would be the ideal place. My grandsons, staying with us on holiday from England, were impressed.

At regular intervals I checked the cage by lifting it out of the water, and on one occasion I found a white fish in it. But no crayfish. After three days the white fish had somehow got away and still no crayfish had decided to experience the comfort of the cage.

It was lifted out of the water before we flew back to England in autumn, empty and sad. I checked with a variety of people whether the cage had been assembled correctly, and they all agreed that it was perfect. I still hate those friends of ours who claim that by simply dropping such a cage into the water, they manage to catch fish. I have never managed to get an explanation from any of them as to why they are successful and I am not. I just hate them, and I do not believe them. Or I hate myself for being so useless when it comes to fishing.

So our opinion of Finnish food is excellent when it is traditional and does not just consist of burgers and chips or bread and cakes. Many of the cookery programs on television are now encouraging people to go back to basics and discover that the old cheap dishes are a delicacy and can also be fashionable today. Fashion does not come into it. Tradition does. Sometimes it feels good to defy cholesterol and high blood pressure—something modern society has become so obsessive about—and just feel naughty. The taste is good and, as always, we may be dead tomorrow.

• • • • • •

Every year in July the season of art exhibitions starts. Even in small villages such as ours. There seems to be a proliferation of artists. Some are serious and schooled, but most are self-trained and enthusiastic. All of them open up their houses and gardens or take up space in libraries, schools and village halls and show their works with great pride.

We have been to a great number of such shows, and we have mostly met the same visitors year after year. It is almost like a regimented circuit which people want to belong to, even if they are not really interested in paintings or sculptures. It is something that has to be done, because local art is another unifying element of the Finnish culture, albeit with a short history that goes back only to the late nineteenth century, when the likes of Sibelius, Kallela, Wickstrom, and Halonen started producing their innovative masterpieces, some from their impressive studios with wonderful views of inspiring lakes.

Finnish art history is as short as the nation's history. Nothing happened until the late nineteenth century, when suddenly a number of politically motivated and comfortably rich men started living like the Great Gatsby, building impressive studios and homes, spending time together drinking and generally having fun, but also creating their paintings, their sculptures, their music, and their buildings. Their wealthy, decadent, and hedonistic way of life seems to reflect that of wealthy socialites during the first two decades of the last century the world over. Halonen seems to be the exception. The father of eight children and struggling through his early years because of his humble origins, he made it to Paris and to international recognition after producing a massive numbers of works and without ever joining the libertines.

They all had many children, often from more than one wife, and some even exchanged wives with their working partners, like the famous architect and designer Saarinen who, with two colleagues, built a remarkable set of English-looking houses at Hvitresk on the outskirts of Espoo in a forest near Helsinki. All shared parties, tennis matches, dinners, and wives. All of them took an active role in the politics of the time, choosing between the Whites and the Reds, the two factions that supported respectively the democratic government and the Russian regime. They felt part of the evolving Finnish scene and took a great interest in Freemasonry, which appeared to many intellectuals as the unifying and liberating motif. Kallela even injected some of the symbolism into his paintings, as mentioned earlier.

Every one of the exhibitions offers free coffee and cakes, and this is an irresistible attraction for the Finns. They do love their coffee, and they drink an awful lot of it, but they love it even more when it is free, be it at an art event or at the opening of a new shop.

A friend of ours has an elegant gift and furniture shop in the nearby town, and on some occasions such as the start of a new franchise or the tenth anniversary of the business, she advertises in the local newspaper her small reception to which everyone is welcome, starting from a certain time in the morning and at which coffee and cakes will be offered to visitors. It is a nice little promotional and public relations exercise. I mentioned earlier how punctual the Finns always are, and on these occasions they can even be a little early, eagerly waiting for the shop doors to open and diving towards the table where the pot of hot coffee and some cakes are waiting. According to our friend, only a minority takes any interest in the products on show. Most have a couple of coffees and a few cakes and then leave, maybe with a just a single "goodbye".

So they go to art exhibitions, one after the other, on a kind of timetable that reminds me of the stereotypical American family visiting European cities: "Today is Tuesday, so it must be Berlin because we were in Paris yesterday." At the end of the day, with a belly full of coffee and cakes and none the wiser about works of art, they go home, heat up their saunas, and have a beer and a sausage feeling that they have done their duty.

Certainly for a nation of little more than three million adults, Finland has a remarkable number of art galleries and museums, religiously visited by almost everyone, all succeeding in ensuring that the Finns never forget their past and never stop feeling Finnish with pride.

Some of the "museums" are not much more than simple old wooden farmhouses that have decided to put on show the ancestors' working tools. Others are beautifully conserved entire city quarters, where the wooden houses and the working places remind us of the ways and conditions of a not too distant past. A good example is the wonderful area in Turku, in which some of the workshops are still used by artisans and where a well-produced guide leaflet takes you through the stages of progress of working families over the past century.

Some museums are almost places of veneration and pilgrimage. They stand as milestones of the artistic development of the nation, as well as being impressively built monuments to artists who had the passion, the courage, and the finances to live differently and to leave a mark in Finnish culture. Among these I must no doubt mention again the imposing working places of Kallela and Wickstrom. Both of their houses and studios, built on high and rocky peninsulas that seem to cut through the lakes down below, are worth seeing just for their design and location, let alone for the art pieces that they contain. These are valuable works from minds that lived and breathed the new aspirations and political turmoil of the infant Finnish society and that for the first time put Finland on the world's art map.

Once on our way back from attending a performance of Verdi's Aida in the island castle of Savonlinna (at the yearly great cultural feast put up by Finland), we made a little detour and visited Retretti, one of the best-known art exhibition centres in the country. It was a hot summer's day, and we had some difficulty in parking the car in the shade, as the place was full of visitors. Savonlinna's opera season in July brings visitors from all parts of the world, and most of them spread to many areas in the south-eastern half of Finland, reaching also Retretti, only a few kilometres away. For us that year was the first visit to Savonlinna. A couple of friends took us there, showing us a few things on the way, like the fighting line with the Russian army during the Winter Wars, the Russian border along the Old Karelian Way, Imatra, Lappeenranta, and the famous Saima Lake with all its islands and ferries and coves.

Savonlinna is a lovely little town by the shores of Saimaa, the largest of the Finnish lakes. It more than doubles its small population during the opera season, and no one has much chance of getting a reasonable accommodation that does not look like a Spartan student room. On our second visit we ended up staying in a place where our bedroom consisted of two small beds, two small bedside tables, and a window, all on bare floor tiles. We had a couple of towels too. The two or three decent hotels in the town are booked one year ahead and cannot cater for the invasion of visitors and music enthusiasts from many parts of the world. After our second attendance we decided to give Savonlinna a miss, despite the fact that we seriously enjoyed both the performances and the atmosphere.

The opera house itself has been created out of the courtyard of the old Island Castle a few hundred metres from the mainland, reached by a mobile bridge that occasionally has to be opened to let large boats and ships get to the main harbour through the only small stretch of deep waters. Walking along the bridge to the castle in the warm early evening breeze together with hundreds of other people, you cannot but feel that Savonlinna is perceived as a kind of Finnish version of Ascot – elegant, classy, and exclusive.

When we saw Aida, it was the opening night of the season, and the Finnish President was attending. At the end of the evening we found ourselves walking back to the mainland along the bridge with everyone else exiting the castle, including the President. Mrs Halonen was walking surrounded by some of her ministers and undoubtedly some inconspicuous body guards, far from the obsessive security measures we have been used to in our country. At the end of the bridge only two black cars were waiting for her and her entourage, aerials protruding through the roofs and the bulky drivers wearing the give-away sunglasses and holding mobile phones. Nothing more. After all, the President was surrounded by her own people. Who should want to harm her?

So the following day our friends took us to Retretti, after a short stop in Kerimaki to visit the world's largest wooden church, with its imposing structure. A christening was just about to start, and the place was full of flowers. The intricate structure of the naves and pillars was impressive, and the pastel colours of the wood carvings were simply perfect.

Retretti had neatly kept lanes sided by tall trees that led to a modern building designed with plenty of glass in mind. The leaflets and catalogues by the entrance were in a variety of languages and headphones were also available on request to hear the usual impersonal voice explain the history of the place and the works on exhibit. Many famous Finnish artists are featured regularly, together with other examples of Finnish creativity. The underground section, excavated through hard rocks deep in the bowels of Retretti, showed unusual and innovative experiments with lights and visual effects, as well as various collections of objects, from crazy and generally useless inventions to precious stones and the skeletons of rare animals. I was taken by the care that Retretti's experts showed towards anything that is Finnish and by the imagination used to create a mixed and unique exhibition. In fact, after our visit, we found that some of the concepts adopted at Retretti have subsequently been imported by other countries' museums.

Retretti is another of the many "compulsory" visits that the Finns make through the country to keep themselves attached to Finnish history and to maintain their pride in this small nation's intellect and ability of expression. Arts unite them. In recent years there were suggestions that Retretti might close down because of lack of funds and sponsorship; I must admit that I was rather horrified at the prospect of Finland losing such a wonderful showcase for its artists and craftsmen. Then suddenly funds seemed to be found and a lifeline was thrown to this very good establishment, which would have been greatly missed by many art lovers.

I was certainly more impressed by Retretti than I was by Ittala, another household name, that lies between Tampere and Hammenliina. Ittala is a glorified glass maker, most of whose pieces have had their time and have now become supermarkets' and even cheap shops' shelf merchandise. Nonetheless, these pieces still seem to maintain an image of sophistication and design quality in the Finnish perception.

At Ittala visitors can see how glass is blown and shaped, but they can also see how chocolate cakes are made. They can buy Chinese-made Finnish souvenirs and can have hamburgers in the small coffee shop by the car park. They can walk into a small building where on two floors and over a large number of tiny rooms, they can view the most extravagant mismatch of paintings, prints, caricatures, sculptures, photographs, and the like. There are so many pieces crammed on show that it is impossible to remember what you have seen and where. But again, people flock to Ittala, to this open circus, as to something that has to be seen, part of the Finnish art heritage. And coffee and cakes are not even free!

• • • • • •

The Finns are decidedly formal when it comes to congregations and gatherings.

As in all Protestant communities, the act of going to service is almost an organized ritual rather than a spontaneous expression. Notice the great difference between a service in a Catholic church and a Protestant one. In the former, people seem to feel free to walk about, arrive late, chat, enter and exit at liberty, take Communion, and bump into others who are waiting to take it. Children make noises, scream, and run around. (Mind you, nowadays embarrassed parents are not legally allowed to tell children off anywhere in case the poor little ones develop complexes.) It is generally a shambles.

Protestant services are almost regimented. The congregation is punctual and quiet. They sit still, and even the children suddenly lose their desire to walk about or laugh. Generally the whole congregation takes Communion, and people organize themselves in two distinct lines, both with stern and serious faces, one moving towards the vicar or pastor, and one moving away, neatly and silently, after taking the holy bread and wine. Everything functions like clockwork.

The Finns do not talk much about religion. It is a personal affair between the individual and God; it is not something to joke about or to fight for. Other creeds than Lutheranism are accepted and respected but not discussed. People are taken for what they are and certainly not for what their beliefs are. Even the small Jewish or Islamic communities live side by side in Finland with no extreme feelings. Finland is a country of forests, and in the forests – like it or not – everyone is really equal in the eyes of bears and elks.

Years ago a couple of friends suggested that we should join them for an early Christmas Day service in the nice wooden village church with its steep roof and adjoining bell tower. I decided to let Celia have a rest after all the preparations and cooking for the festivities. Our friend picked me up at a ridiculously early morning hour when the light of day was still very far away. The church was packed with worshippers who had fought with snow and ice on their way to the service. It was a lovely Christmas occasion, and I did enjoy being part of the community, listening to the simple and serious sermon by the pastor, and exchanging wishes with members of the congregation on the way home to a hot coffee. Everything had been perfect – no noises, no sneezes, no coughing. God was respected by silence and order.

But Finns are formal at every gathering, even among close friends, until coffee and cakes are served. Once in the church for a service, they are serious and acknowledge the presence of a friend only by imperceptibly bowing the head. Once the service is over, they go back to being their friendly jovial selves. All gatherings are to be treated with respect and formality.

I remember when Celia and I were asked to join Veikko at his lovely family home in the forest for his sixtieth birthday. We were given a time, of course, and we made a point of not being late. It was a lovely warm day in early summer, and after parking the car on the dry cut grass of an adjacent field, we walked the short distance towards the house. We saw a number of people waiting in a line in the farmyard, and we looked out for Veikko and his gentle wife Marjatta. They are a lovely friendly couple who own a vast expanse of land in one of the areas within our village boundaries. It is a community of its own, with its "Mayor" and "Sheriff", and it keeps very much alive the spirit of the village within a village. It is still a small tribe today as it was in ancient times, be it with cars and telephones and internet rather than horns and foot messengers.

When we spotted them, Veikko and Mariatta were standing not far from the main house, being congratulated by guests. We went to them and exchanged greetings and birthday wishes, undoubtedly joking about Veikko's age. Only at that moment did we realize with horror that we had in fact jumped the queue. Those people in a line were one by one moving towards Veikko to express their wishes and offering small presents, and we should have taken our place at the back of the queue. That is the system. We felt rude and embarrassed, and I think we even blushed, me under my beard, as if we had let the whole of Britain down. For a short moment we would have liked to make the proverbial hole in the ground and disappear. We were not told off, of course, and the gentle smiles that we received even from unknown people made us feel even worse.

It was a lesson for us. At any gathering you have to patiently wait for your turn to express thanks and salutations to the host, in a composed line, perhaps even waiting for the people before you to give short speeches of friendship to the host. Formalities are important. It is the same when you walk into a room – for example the singing sessions at Aulikki's - where others are already sitting around the tupa. We know that we have to walk round the room, shaking each hand and introducing ourselves to everyone, even to people we already know. Formalities are important. And yet, men do not stand when ladies are introduced to them … Once the formalities are over and the coffee is served with the inevitable cakes, the stern and serious faces disappear and Finns become once again jolly and funny. They relax.

It is a kind of ritual you have to go through. On Eino Einol's day in early Summer (a famous national poet), Eino, an artist friend of ours who shares his name and birth date with the famous man, takes the opportunity to celebrate both occasions. Eino and his wife Pirkko live (as you know by now) in the forest in a lovely old house with a great natural garden. Among the rocks are some of Eino's sculptures, witty, different, and extravagant, from fat ladies with funny noses to caricatures of politicians. At one end of the garden Pirkko grows vegetables, nicely lined up and always looking healthy. Their garden ends at the forest beyond the red outbuildings, where Hanna, their first small dog, was not allowed to go for danger of being swallowed by wolves. Hanna has since passed away, and Eino celebrated her with a small sculpture that stands in the garden.

On his fiftieth birthday Eino asked us to join a few friends at his house for a small celebration, and we decided that an appropriate gift

– also in view of the coincidence with the famous literate's birthday – would be a short poem dedicated to him. I have often dabbled in rhymes for sheer enjoyment and personal pleasure, so I had fun in writing a few sestines (obviously in English), which I printed out on an A4 sheet. Once rolled and tied with a red string, the document looked impressive and almost like an ancient Roman papyrus.

When we arrived at Eino's place and parked the car, we found a small queue of friends already lined up to pay homage to the host, along the path leading to his studio. It was a warm summer's day, and Eino and Pirkko were standing together, receiving their guests and patiently listening to all the words of praise and appreciation for Eino's character and artistic successes. Some sang short tunes to him, while others handed over small gifts. Everyone was made very welcome.

When our turn came, Celia gave Eino a small present and I unrolled the "poem" and read it out to him slowly, trying to allow him to understand the meaning of the words, even with his limited knowledge of English. I was pleased to see Pirkko, whose command of English is good, occasionally smiling at the witty rhymes. Then we moved on along the path to where coffee and cakes were offered, leaving the next person to fulfil his or her friendly duty towards Eino. Not until everyone who had arrived had been welcomed did Eino and Pirkko join the gathering. It was another human experience of Finnish ways – simple, genuine, warm, and formal.

Eino and Pirkko are genuine and natural themselves. Everyone likes them. Even our grandchildren clearly feel comfortable with them, as they are treated in the usual genuine and sincere way by our friends. One day Luke, our younger grandson, was extremely impressed by Eino's patience and care when, after spending some time at their cottage one Summer afternoon, eating cakes that Pirkko had prepared, he was taken out to the garden to collect some worms that apparently would be the best of bait for fishing on Paijanne. Both children, Joseph and Luke, are quite keen on fishing – a passion clearly inherited from their father. We had bought them a couple of inexpensive fishing rods at the village service station. I know nothing about fishing, and the rods seemed okay to me.

Eino had already given the children some suggestions while we sat around the table in the kitchen as to the best way of fishing with success. Then he waved Luke to follow him outside, and after a short while the artist and our grandson came back into kitchen with a jar half full of long fat wiggly brown worms that sent shivers down Celia's spine. Celia has a dislike and almost an allergy for any creature with no legs, and worms are the best possible proof of her phobia.

Once he was back at our place, Luke felt it necessary to write a thank-you card to Eino. This read, "Thank you, Eino, very much for the worms and the cakes." Somehow we could see where Luke's priorities seemed to lay.

• • • • • •

Sarah, our younger daughter, and her (now) husband were spending some time with us one summer. The weather had been beautiful for them, and every day we had been able to enjoy our garden and the lake and take a few small trips across the country, rich with shades of green and blue and full of birds and berries.

One afternoon we visited a remote country house, standing alone in its pale pastel colours on a low hill that descended rapidly to a small pretty lake with a narrow path ending by a wooden sauna. The place belonged to a lady we had seen on some occasions in the village and who had decided to retire from her employment as a supermarket assistant. She had started a little business weaving carpets, mats, and garments and had transformed the beautiful outbuildings around the square grassy yard into basic but fashionable showrooms, where her handicrafts were on display, together with some paintings by local amateur artists. It was an idyllic place, and we were made very welcome.

On the way back we decided to make a detour and stop for a drink at a bar by the small harbour of a village on a nearby lake. It certainly was a small harbour. A single fishing boat was moored, and it took up almost the entire jetty. An old man arrived in a patched-up rowing boat with an engine at the back and a dog standing at the front. It looked like a scene out of the famous American gold rush. He left the boat in the dry mud of the shore and went, with the dog, for a drink.

The bar was a wooden barn with some tables and seats at one end and a children's play area on a kind of raised decking at the other. On the wall above the children's area were a variety of axes, hunters' knives, saws, and other horrible-looking country objects. They were just hanging from the wall as decorations. Sarah, who is a Norland nanny and knows a thing or two about babies and children and their safety, almost had an immediate heart attack at the possibility that one of the objects might fall on the children while they were playing, or even that one of the children might get too interested in one of the tools and decided to try and get it. There were no signs warning parents and children to be aware of the danger and no safety nets or guards to ensure that no harm would be done.

Children have obviously been playing in that area for ever, while their parents have had a meal or a drink. Apparently, no child has ever been killed by the tools or has even attempted to get hold of them, and the children's attention has never been drawn to them by overanxious parents conscious that any accident would give them grounds for suing and compensation. I am sure Big Brother and the compensation culture will reach even Finland one day. For now it is refreshing to know that such culture is still miles and years away.

This is something that we have seen with great regularity. There are no "mind your head" or "mind the step" signs. The principle is that if you trip or hit your head on a beam, you will be careful not to do it again. It's as simple as that – just an unfortunate small accident.

The thing is that Finns are so close to nature that they grow up with the concept that accidents do happen, and in most cases they are just accidents. An elk might run through a window of a house in a wood, not realizing with its poor eyesight that it is not an open space and that the trees it sees in the window are just a reflection of the wood in the glass. People might fall through the ice of a frozen lake. These things just happen, and people do not even imagine that they can claim compensation from the forestry commission or from the local council for not providing sufficient information on how elks go about forests or on the instability of thin ice.

The Finn's seem to have a philosophical acceptance of events, particularly when they are the result of Mother Nature. We have been told by friends that almost every family has someone who has either just fallen through the thin ice into the frozen lake waters or has even died by disappearing under the icy surface, never to be found. This was told to us with no intention to shock us, but with the casuality of something inevitable that everyone in this country has to face, thanks to nature and maybe to the Finn's hidden desire to often try the extreme.

Recently Finland experienced the most impressive and persistent snowfall in the last forty years – so we were told – and the thickness of the snow reached dangerous levels on the roofs of buildings. The snow was fluffy and dry for many months, but a rise in temperature followed by freezing conditions meant that the weight became a worry. The Minister for Housing declared that the danger of roofs collapsing, especially in large public buildings with flat roofs, was too great to be overlooked and suggested that people should be careful to remove the snow.

With typical Finnish diligence and with respect for authority's directives, on one weekend almost everyone could be seen on rooftops shovelling snow off tiles and corrugated iron roofs. The result was that hundreds of people ended up in hospital with broken legs and a variety of other serious injuries after sliding off the roofs. At the news of the accidents the same minister was heard to say, "Of course, people should use their common sense when removing the snow."

At school as a young child, you are taught how to cope with the ice, which usually covers the country for half the year, and how to roll flat on the surface to impose as little pressure as possible on the precarious support offered by the frozen water. After that you may take precautions, you might purchase a pair of gripped handles that can be bought in shops all over the country that would give some help in lifting yourself out of the freezing water, or alternatively you might decide not go out at all. It's your choice.

We have seen these handles. They have a spiky tip and a string attached to each end. You can carry them around your neck just in case. Most shops start selling them by October, and I have often pictured the unfortunate (or silly) individual who decides to walk over some hundreds of metres of water, supported by ice, and falls through a weak spot. His (or her) body is immersed in sub-zero temperature, his feet are dangling in dark water, his head is constantly hitting the ice above, and his hands are trying desperately to get a grip on the ice edges to enable him to raise his whole body back onto the solid ice. The thought of getting the pair of handles from around my neck and lifting my head above water in an effort to survive terrifies me. The thought of my legs floating under the ice and making it impossible for me to keep my strength as I attempt to pull my weight out of the freezing hole, makes me shiver – literally. But Finns seem to accept it as a fact of life.

We have been on the frozen lake many times, walking, sledging, and admiring the beauty of nature around us. But before venturing onto the ice, we have always waited until we see cars, tractors, and skiers tempting fate first, and we always check with our native and expert neighbours before walking out in comfort and with peace of mind.

Accidents do happen, and Finns just accept it. Our neighbour Jorma, with his long-established fishing business, knows the lake even better than the back of his hand. His knowledge of every corner and crevice of the lake is unique. He could find his way around the many islands dotting Paijanne blindfolded or in the middle of the darkest night.

One day Jorma went out on his skidoo pulling a trailer, probably with the intention of checking some of the fishing nets that in winter he puts into the water through holes in the ice. From our kitchen window we saw him driving across the small section of Paijanne towards the open lake. He went around the corner of the island opposite us, and we lost sight of him. It had not been an extremely cold winter, with the ice covering the water surface but never becoming thicker than a few centimetres.

Jorma's knowledge of every corner and crevice of the lake is unique but on his way back he apparently went over a particularly thin patch of ice, and his skidoo and trailer sank miserably into the depths of the lake. He managed to throw himself off the sinking vehicle and roll towards the shore and was driven back home over land by a nearby friend.

We met him shortly after the incident, and we mentioned our horror at the danger that he must have faced. He was relaxed and smiling about the whole thing. It had caused him no real reason for distress or shock. He simply told us that it happened and that he would try to get his skidoo out of the water at some point in the future when the lake was liquid again. End of story.

It is certainly not a form of fatalism. It is a wonderful acceptance of events that are part of this country's culture and habitat. No wonder that if you trip on an uneven paving stone while walking along a pavement, you do not even imagine that you could sue anyone.

Finns seem to have a refreshingly candid approach to life and business. In most countries people supposedly employed to assist and help become obnoxious examples of arrogance and intolerance; they appear in fact to be working against their will and simply sit and philosophise about the meaning of existence, whilst every person who needs their services becomes a complete nuisance to them. In Finland the concept of everyone belonging to the same small country is prevailing and staff in offices – public or not – genuinely want to help. The personal touch is still there. The personal interest is still there.

I could mention a number of cases that directly concerned us, relating to the electricity company, to Sonera (the telephone company), or to Sampo (the insurance company), where queries were dealt with by a person and not by a "call centre" in India or Timbuktu, and were sorted out swiftly and pleasantly, and certainly more economically than when the telephone call has to last for an excessive amount of time simply because the "advisor" (as they are called nowadays) cannot understand the language.

In Finland matters are handled by people who know Finland and not by people sitting in an office block in Mumbai, for whom in most cases a property ladder is the ownership of a set of steps and inflation is the blowing up of a plastic doll for a randy old man.

• • • • • •

One thing that struck us right from the start about the Finns is their perception of work.

Work is something that has to be done to occupy one's time and to procure sufficient funds for people to enjoy their saunas, their boats, their holidays, and their sausages, but work can very often be an interference with life, an uncomfortable duty, and every possible reason is found to avoid it at regular intervals.

The comfort of a socialist democracy where the income tax has always been high, but the benefits to the taxpayer are very high too, seems to have created a relaxed approach to work and the consequent desire to take every opportunity to alternate work with pleasure in the knowledge that the security of a job is always there. At least this was the case until recently, when the bite from the global crisis on the work force has become very unpleasant even in this country.

I remember a simple episode of many years ago on a warm late summer evening, when Celia and I were standing on the edge of our jetty that stretched into the waters of Paijanne, admiring the colour of the lake and the wonderful forests around us.

A small motor boat approached from the middle of the lake, and Irja, Pekka, and family came to say hello to us. We asked them to tie the boat to one of the rings at the corner of our jetty and have a drink with us in the garden. Irja discretely put a robe around her bikini and stepped out of the boat with Pekka and their children and introduced us to their passenger, whom the children called uncle. He was Irja's brother. We spent the next hour or so enjoying a gin and tonic and a beer in the dimming light of the evening, sitting around a table on the grass outside our back door.

The company was pleasant and the evening comfortably warm. Some mosquitos were dancing around the lights as the evening became darker and darker, and their pale glow made our shadows extend to impossible dimensions. When the time came for our guests to go, "uncle" expressed his disappointment at having to go to work in the morning after such a good weekend, and having considered the matter for a few moments decided that in fact he might not go into work at all, since he did not have very much to do anyway and his boss would understand. The lake, the forests, the summer, the boat, the drinks … all were much more interesting than working.

Not very often I have come across this kind of boss.

I remember a lovely old wooden house right in the middle of the village that was suddenly occupied some time ago by an antique store. One moment the building was empty, and the following moment it opened its door to reveal a collection of old furniture, paintings, farm objects, china sets, trunks, and the like. We visited it a few times, and we even bought some pieces that at the time appeared suitable for our house. Some we still have, others have been given away or have been thrown away. We became friends with the owner, a petite red-haired young lady called Sari, who happened to have rented a house not too far from us, at the very end of the island.

After only one full summer of trading, Sari announced that she was abandoning her antique business. She was moving to Lahti, a major city some ninety kilometres away. She had had enough of the village environment and wanted to enjoy a more adventurous life in a larger place. She had no idea what job to take up. We could only wish her luck.

One year later we saw her again in the village on a Saturday during the traditional summer market. Sari had worked in Lahti for a few weeks and then decided that she might prefer to leave and work in the more inspiring Helsinki, and she had found a job with an insurance company. She was not sure whether she liked the work and how long she might stay in the employment. We could only wish her luck, again.

A number of our friends, all middle-aged and married, or committed to a partner, have at different times decided to take a year off work and return to college or university to obtain degrees in various subjects. Their reasons were strangely similar. "I need to take a break from work and study again to feel that I am achieving something." The fact is that after their sabbatical they walked straight back into their old jobs, which had been kept for them for the duration of their studies. Apart from probably feeling fulfilled, they never seemed to make any use of their newly acquired degrees or diplomas.

Work seems to be a kind of inconvenient interlude between the things that people really like doing, like picking mushrooms or sailing in the summer or skiing or walking through forests or doing nothing. Sometimes they like to sit and think, and other times they just like to sit – of course, at a rather great cost for the country.

The social system now seems to have finally realized that the relaxed approach to work and the facilities provided to workers by the state can no longer be afforded; the tune is slowly changing, and there are more stringent regulations on unemployment benefits. After all, there are too few tax-payers in a country with an adult population of just over three million and with a vast empty territory that still needs servicing, caring, protecting, developing and that most of all must fulfil its commitments to the infamous European Union's treasure box.

Paijanne

This massive lake stretches some 180 kilometres from south to north, right in the middle of Finland's "tummy". From Lahti to Jyvaskyla (one of the most amazing names to pronounce correctly, while people constantly make you aware of your mistakes), like a long and wide cut in the Finnish countryside, it seemingly takes care of the thousands of smaller lakes in central Finland.

Paijanne is not the largest lake in the country. That prerogative belongs to Saimaa, an immense water basin in south-eastern Finland, with a convoluted coastline that makes you feel as if you are seeing an immense number of different lakes, all somehow interconnected with bridges and ferries and blotted by innumerable islands.

Paijanne is however the oldest and the deepest of the Finnish lakes. Its origins go back to the ice age, when what is now known as Finland was a mass of perennial ice. It is also supposedly the cleanest, its water even being fed to Helsinki via a manmade canal for the capital city to have sufficient drinking provision. Someone once told us – with tongue in cheek – that if you pee into Paijanne in Jyvaskyla, someone in Helsinki sooner or later will drink your discharge. He was joking of course, but when we are in Helsinki we make a point of drinking only bottled mineral water. Just in case.

Paijanne is a paradise for birds and birdwatchers, and because of its depth, some of the rarest specimens of fishing and diving birds have their home on its waters. We often admire from our kitchen window grebes and their babies going for an early morning swim on the placid lake. Constantly talking among themselves with their typical little shrieks, they disappear under water every now and then in a quick diving motion. Grebes are larger than ducks and carry themselves in the water with an air of aristocracy, their plumed black head turning from side to side before each dive, which may last several seconds and cover tens of metres under water. They are shy birds, rarely ashore, and it is rewarding to see them occasionally resting on our jetty or at the end of our garden.

Even black-throated divers at times find the courage to snooze on our wooden jetty, standing in their funny upright position because their legs are so far back under their body. These are very rare birds, apparently unique to Paijanne, which, thanks to its depth that reaches over 100 metres in some parts, offers them an ideal habitat, where they can spend time and enjoy long swims under water even without respirators. They are large beautiful timid birds, and we feel privileged to see them by our house.

Golden-eye ducks are also commonly seen on Paijanne, as are the more traditional ducks, which often in the summer bring their ducklings almost up to our front door in search of some crumbs. Every year a family of Canadian geese makes its appearance. Though they are beautiful, calm, and rather majestic on water, swimming with their elongated necks upright, they are a menace to every house by the lake where they happen to rest for the night. Their droppings are in such quantity and size that it almost looks as if a colony of human invaders took residence after some hefty meals.

Swans and seagulls are regular inhabitants too. The former gently swim in couples or with cygnets, strangely silent after sounding their deep trumpets in flight before landing with big splashes on the water like white planes. The latter constantly scream in acute falsetto, especially when their babies are placed on our jetty by the parents with strict orders not to move. Young seagulls always look sad and miserable, not yet able to stand proud like their elders. When we dare walk around the garden and young seagulls are on the jetty, we are often threatened by their protective parents, who dive towards us screaming, like noisy acrobats of the sky.

Unusual creatures can also be seen on Paijanne. I remember a few years back looking out on the lake from our windows and being puzzled by what seemed a dark frightening object floating past our house. Somehow it did not look normal. It was certainly no boat and no human. With the help of a pair of binoculars, I discovered that the "Loch Ness Paijanne Monster" was in fact an elk, happily swimming within our section of the lake, from one side to the other. Its large antlers looked black and scary, and its head was just above the water surface. It went past, apparently knowing its destination, swimming with great ease and looking at the same time calm and menacing. We were glad that we had not encountered the animal while out on the lake rowing in our little boat. It would not have been a relaxing meeting. We were tempted to run out of the house and stand by the edge of the lake waving at the beast, shouting a few salutations, but we stayed in the house so as not to frighten the floating animal, knowing that elks do not speak English.

Elks, despite their considerable size and the spread of their antlers can move at ease through thick forests with no noise and without bumping their head against trees. Once, while on an expedition to see available properties in the country with a local estate agent, I had to stop the car for a call of nature. I made myself invisible by climbing the wooded bank and hiding behind trees. When I went back to the car, Celia and Kurt were laughing and pointing at the spot where I had just been. Apparently they had seen a bull elk coming up to me from behind, so close that they were certain he was sniffing my back. I had heard or seen nothing.

Paijanne has an abundance of fish, including pike, white fish, bream, trout, salmon, and a variety of others that I cannot even name with my poor knowledge of the fish community, but that I have seen in Jorma's catch and have even enjoyed eating. They are good healthy fish, despite some people's fears still persisting about the fact that the famous Chernobyl disaster in 1986 in the Ukraine may have affected the lake water, poisoning it to this day.

Paijanne is an exceedingly beautiful lake, on which the thousands of small islands are the welcome retreat for so many people whose summer cottages enjoy the solitude and the peace of Finnish life at its best. I shall never forget when Iris and Juhani still had a cottage on one such small island and asked us to join them for a simple evening meal of fish and potatoes and to admire both the sun and the moon on the opposite sides of the lake. We were taken there in their motor boat, and over a beer and some boiled fish, we enjoyed a most breath-taking sight. The orange sun was diving into Paijanne in the west, and the bright moon was appearing on the other side of the island in the east. Both sun and moon were of immense size. It was certainly worth the thirty-minute boat trip.

When we first started coming to our house on Paijanne, the jetty was a small wooden platform, held afloat by large black rigid plastic tubes. It cannot have been more than four square metres in size, but despite its lack of stability and its dependence on the size and power of the waves produced by passing boats, we used to spend hours on it, soaking up the sunshine on tiny canvas chairs, enjoying food and drinks off a minuscule round metal table. I am certain that people on boats must have thought of us as a mad middle-aged couple, and if they ever knew we were English, we must have represented in their eyes the ultimate example of English eccentricity.

It was fun. Paijanne in the summer is always busy with sailing and motor boats, with the police power boat often hovering in the middle of the lake. They check the speed of the crafts leaving and approaching the village and often stop them to check documents and probably the alcohol intoxication level of the pilots. It was all new to us, and we enjoyed every minute. Now after many years, everything has become familiar, and we do not even bother to wave at boats – especially since, years ago, we took the frantic waving of arms of a gentleman in a small motorboat opposite our house as friendly gestures of greetings. We did not realize that in fact the poor man was in trouble; his engine broken down. We had never felt so silly.

It was also at this time when a few things were lost in Paijanne. Things like my glasses, for example. I went for a swim one day and had started descending the steps from the jetty into the water, when Celia called out at me, pointing at something. I immersed myself into the water only to realize that I had kept my glasses on and they were now gently floating away from me. It was too late to retrieve them. They slowly and miserably sank into the depths of Paijanne.

Fortunately I had a spare set – an old frame reminiscent of the glasses of Hank, the guitarist in the sixties band the Shadows. For some time and until I managed to get another set from Boots back at home, I went around looking like a tortoise-shell blind man.

On another occasion Celia and I decided to have some champagne on the jetty, drinking to Finland and the sunshine. After filling our first glass I thought – with a touch of genius – to keep the bottle cool by placing it on some stones in the water. Not a clever idea. The bottle stood for about three seconds, before being pushed by the water's gentle waves and disappearing to the bottom of the lake.

Then there was the time when I was standing on the jetty, in bright sunshine, with our cordless telephone in the pocket of my trousers, ready to take that all-important call from my office that might change our lives. I have no idea what happened next. I fell off the jetty and into Paijanne, fully dressed. And I cannot even say that I had had a whisky too many; it was mid-morning. I climbed back onto the wooden platform, my old-fashioned tortoise-shell glasses still on my face, and I remember my immediate concern being for the telephone handset. I took it out of my pocket and in my brilliant naivety I placed it on the jetty in the sun, believing that by drying it off it might still work. It did not, of course, and we had to buy another telephone.

And I remember when a similar incident occurred sometime later, when I had improved my technology skills and got myself a mobile phone. This allowed me to be in contact with my business at any time, forgetting about normal house and public telephones. I could be in touch with things wherever I might happen to be, even on our jetty on a lake in the middle of Finland. So there was I on our wobbly jetty, proudly holding my mobile phone in one hand, when an inexplicable movement of the jetty made me drop my Motorola flip phone into the water. My technology pride was gone for ever into the depths of Paijanne. I stood motionless watching the black phone gently sinking, with an almost teasing smile on its screen. I had visions of a sizeable pike sitting on Paijanne's sandy bottom, wearing my glasses, drinking my champagne, and talking to his friends on my mobile phone!

The time had come when something had to be done about the jetty.

Some of the visitors' boats, especially during the July holiday, when the cities of Helsinki, Espoo, Porvoo, and others pour their inhabitants onto the lakes of central Finland. These people do not seem able to have any consideration for "peasants" like us and the other local country people. They drive so close to the shores that the concertino waves from their hulls and from their at times irrational speed disrupt the jetties and the coast. They can be seen in the village supermarkets, often with their noses up in the air, pushing their way through the locals with complete disregard for what they seem to consider a kind of inferior race. They drive their powerful boats in the same way, standing on the open top, high up in the sky, looking down at everyone else, especially at us in our small green rowing boat with no engine, and ignoring the fact that their wake treats our little vessel with no mercy.

The floating jetty was changed to a larger and more stable one, one with proper legs fixed to the bottom of the lake. But a larger jetty also meant that more birds could land and rest on it late at night and first thing in the morning, so the first job of the day for me became washing the boards from the their colourful droppings that reveal their complete diet.

Mind you, Paijanne does not have only my things on its sandy bottom. Pekka is a friend and a passionate musician. He plays the piano and the piano accordion, and he has a small band that entertains at parties, weddings, and birthdays. In his large apartment, where his wife Irja is ever hoping to get a new kitchen, Pekka has an upright piano with the facility for blocking the sound to any audience of friends and family, so that he can enjoy his music through earphones without anyone listening.

Nothing is better than a party on Paijanne in midsummer. People have bonfires on boats, drink through the daylight at night, swim, and have a good time. Pekka is no exception, and with some friends he decided to go for a short boat trip around our corner of Paijanne, taking his accordion along to play some music while on the water.

Midsummer is a difficult time for Finns to count their drinks, and Pekka and his friends must have forgotten their numbers. They fell from the boat into the water, and Pekka saw his beloved accordion miserably sink into unknown depths. So now the famous pike is not only wearing my glasses, drinking my champagne and talking to his friends on my mobile telephone; he is also entertaining his friends with music from Pekka's accordion.

Until a few years ago it was quite usual to see a slow-moving convoy of logs pulled by a motor boat pass our windows and take a very wide bend towards the open lake, on their way to one of the many mills along the lake shores. Some of the world's major paper mills are around Paijanne and they are fed by thousands of tons of logs mostly delivered by trucks from all over the country, but it is always nice to see the logs moved on water in the old-fashioned way, almost in slow motion and silence, bringing back memories of western films seen in smoky cinemas as a child, where logs were pushed along rapids and river falls while the Indians watched from nearby hills.

There are no Indians and no real hills around Paijanne; just beautiful and peaceful forests. But the huge mass of logs, pushed and kept together by small tug boats, is almost a step back in time as well as a step into the environmentally friendly future. There are no rapids to overcome and no enemy arrows to avoid, just a peaceful and clean glide over Paijanne.

On the other hand, the lake can very suddenly change its mood and become a dangerous and aggressive mass of water, when storms build up and explode in all their released power.

I remember once after a sunny day seeing the sky over Paijanne suddenly becoming grey and gloomy, the winds building up and bending the tops of the garden willows, while the windows and doors slammed almost in unison. The inflated dark clouds raced each other in a kind of irrational and frightening dance.

From round the corner of the island opposite us came a large motorboat, white and good-looking, with cabins and, no doubt, passengers on board, who had certainly enjoyed a lovely day out on Paijanne and who were looking forward to a rest and a drink in the village harbour. The boat seemed to be in serious trouble, pushed by the strong waves out of its way and towards our section of the lake. It could not be kept on a straight course and appeared to be totally out of control, just a tiny floating object at the lake's pleasure.

I called Jorma, who on many occasions has rescued stranded vessels on Paijanne's waters, but only Elina, his eldest daughter, was home. She had in fact seen the boat in trouble from her home but, despite having the ability and the courage, at the time she had no licence to drive her father's large fishing boat on her own. So we watched powerless as the vessel was carried by the waves almost to both sides of the lake, more and more towards our shore, until suddenly its engines seemed to grip the water again and take control. We saw it slowly turning towards the village and to the calmer waters of the harbour. Paijanne, the great lake, had just reminded us of its strength.

Like everything else in Finland, Paijanne has two separate lives, each special and very different from the other.

At the end of summer, which in Finland is usually during August, the air somehow changes around the lake. Birds group together, ready to fly off to warmer countries. Large numbers of gulls assemble in the middle of the lake, just waiting for some invisible signal to take off. Myriads of fieldfare land on our grass and peck at whatever food they can find, gathering strength for their long flight ahead. Swans fly away in pairs, their deep trumpet-like voices echoing across the water. Every creature gets ready for the oncoming winter.

Only blue tits, magpies, jays, bullfinches, and woodpeckers seem to remain behind and fight the harshness of winter. They actually have it very easy in our garden, as we regularly fill their little feeding houses with seeds of all kinds. One time we bought some that were described on the plastic bag as giving special energy. We were expecting to see the birds transform themselves into little rockets, shooting off in all directions. They seemed to take even the energetic food in good stride, however, continuing to go off and rest over the lunch hours, only to come back and feed for another daily session until the light fades and evening approaches.

Also the ducks stay behind, unaware that on August 18 at exactly 12.00 noon the duck shooting season starts. On the morning of the famous day, boats begin to move to position with their camouflaged passengers looking menacing in their combat suits. Some of the boats are even camouflaged to melt with the colours of the reeds and plants on the water.

And at exactly 12.00 noon every year we hear the first shots sounding across the lake. For the next two or three hours the shots are intense and frequent, and then they become more intermittent, until dusk when they can be heard only occasionally. The lake then goes into its sleep mode. During the following couple of days some shots can still be heard sporadically, with long intervals between them, until they finally die down. By then the wisest ducks have learnt their lesson and have moved to the safety of the harbour and close to houses, and the less intelligent ones are already in someone's freezer. The story will begin again next year. The shooting season officially still open, but the shooters are gone.

We raise the steps from the end of the jetty; the garden chairs and tables are stored; the pump that collects the lake water and makes it possible for me to fill the wooden bucket for my saunas is disconnected. Children have long gone back to school, and Paijanne somehow seems to lose a lot of its water and get ready for the freeze.

Come November every year, the water sinks to its lowest level, and there seems to be no technical reason for this. The lake just seems to prepare itself for the winter freeze. An air of calm falls over the lake, and it begins to look grey and still as it prepares for the six months of snow and ice. Sections of the lake by the shores are always the first to be covered by a thin layer of ice, which then slowly invades ever larger portions, pushing the water away and transforming everything into a shiny grey immobile surface.

By then the reeds that in summer shelter from view many of the houses scattered along Paijanne's edges are dead and reduced to short dry canes that are soon constricted by the ice. Most of the cottages are empty and locked for winter, their occupants returning perhaps only for the Christmas celebrations or are just simply waiting for the next summer. The light fades quickly and even during the hours of daylight it keeps a dull tone, before darkness takes over completely at an early time.

When winters have been "good" and seriously cold, the ice has thickened quickly well before Christmas, allowing the early snow to settle and brighten the lake surface.

People always seem to wait in anticipation for the ice to be solid enough to go walking on it. Someone is always the first to venture over tens of metres of water, supported only by ice. As I said earlier, the risk is great, but this is the point at which life on the lake begins again. Fishermen appear with their push-along sledges, carrying their tack boxes on the wooden seats. They stop wherever they feel fish are resting, and use the heavy drills, bending over the small round holes with their short rods. Ladies take their dogs for walks on the ice, meeting other villagers; roads are made through the snow to allow cars and skidoos to go to the many islands and often trucks or tractors take materials to some of the island cottages for repair or improvement work, the transport of such materials by vehicles being easier over solid ice than by boats over water in the summer.

The last few winters have not been "good". They always seem to come in cycles and people claim that it has nothing to do with global warming. Whatever the reason, the lake did not properly freeze until well after Christmas, to the disappointment of both children and adults but to the understandable satisfaction of Jorma, whose fishing business has had much longer profitable seasons.

The lack of ice has always meant overall darker winters, since the snow could not settle. Darker winters result in a greater number of people suffering with the form of depression, associated with the absence of light that in Finland is called saad. Luckily we do not suffer to such an extreme, but we ourselves have been missing the frosty brightness of the snow on the lake that even at nighttime produces an almost happy glow, particularly when the sky is clear.

For the last two or three winters we have had to wait until late February before the temperature plummeted to reach minus 30 Celsius and the snow became deep and fluffy. In February the days are already much longer than before Christmas and the light is brighter. When temperatures remain this low for prolonged spells, the thickness of the ice over Paijanne grows up to eighty centimetres and more, enough to hold almost any kind of weight and make drilling a fishing hole almost an impossible task.

Once or twice I even managed to convince Celia to go to the village supermarket by car over the lake rather than by road. There was no real need, of course, as the distance is short in any case, but driving over a frozen lake always feels like something of a special adventure.

One February one of our daughters and her family came to spend some ten days with us for the children to enjoy some skiing. Neil, our son-in-law, was itching to drive the children over the lake. He had, of course, walked over the ice just in front of our house where the water would not be too deep anyway, but where the children had warned him that he should be careful without Grandpa, as if I were the world's expert.

One morning Neil decided to have a go. Some shopping was needed in the village, and he asked me to go with him and the children, intending to give them a surprise on the way back, strangely reassured by me being in the car. At the small marina by the wooden bridge between the mainland and our island there is always a gentle slope leading on to the lake that in Winter becomes a beaten track for cars, skidoos, and the like to get onto the ice and join what we jokingly call "the motorway", the wide stretch in the snow that tractors open up for the traffic of vehicles to safely drive on the frozen surface.

I laughed at the shrieks of excitement from the children when the studded tyres finally gripped the icy surface and the car was on the lake. Neil still seemed to be a little apprehensive, but the enormous thickness of the ice layer was as solid as concrete. He drove for about one mile to the middle of the bay, from which we could see our house in the snow, and he never stopped smiling. The children were for once silent, completely taken by the "Nordic explorer's adventure" that would be recounted back at school to their friends, in Devon. For them it had been something magic – as magic as Finland can be.

The last two winters have been spectacularly beautiful and long – and very, very cold. An amazing amount of snow has fallen on Finland, and temperatures have consistently stayed around the minus 25 Celsius level, occasionally reaching almost minus 40 at night. The snow has been always fluffy, soft, dry, like white dust, impossible to use for snowmen in the garden by our grandsons , as it would not stick and mould,

After months of these arctic conditions even the Finns were beginning to moan and long for some warmer weather. In Helsinki the local council officially declared that they were running out of open areas to unload the snow collected by snowploughs in the city, some of the snow piles having reached almost fourteen metres in height, and they stated that they did not expect the snow to thaw fully even during the oncoming summer. It was almost as if one winter was meeting another. But global warming is ever present, according to the experts.

The corner of Paijanne where we are is a deep inlet, with the village harbour at the end by the old mill. The lake narrows on the way to open waters between the mainland and a huge island opposite our house. Walking in winter along this bottleneck means that either on the way out or on the way back, you have to face the atrociously cold and bitter winds that are channelled through this natural funnel. Even at just minus 20 Celsius, the wind effect makes you feel like you are walking by the North Pole (where I have never been, so it is only my imagination). At minus 30 you have to cover your mouth and nose, and the eyes never stop watering, beaten by the freezing wind that makes the temperature feel like minus 50. Your breath freezes on your clothes. I can easily break off my beard that becomes hard and crispy. Despite all this, you feel clean and healthy – or you die in silence – looking forward to the drink that will be waiting for you back at home. It is pleasant to be away from the bubbling sounds made by the frozen lake because of the air entrapped under the ice that always gives the fear of an imminent explosion of water through the ice – which, of course, never happens, I hope.

And winter has that special time called Christmas. If ever a country fits every romantic and traditional vision of a White Christmas, it is Finland. From Finnair's aircrafts, which carry the logo "The Airline of Father Christmas", to the in-flight food, to the Vantaa airport decorations, the whole country is Christmas. Finland is, after all, the land of Santa Claus.

Hordes of visitors from all over the world bring their children to Lapland and have meetings with Father Christmas, before he leaves for his exhausting journey. In every country there is good television coverage of his departure as he is seen leaving, pulled by his famous Rudolph at the head of a pack of reindeer. One Christmas Eve many years ago, we told one of our grandsons in England that we had seen Father Christmas leave his workshop in Lapland to deliver toys to good children around the world. He remarked on how fast Santa could travel, as it looked as if the stockings had already arrived at his cottage in Devon.

Over Christmas Paijanne comes alive, with the bright lights of the summer cottages that are suddenly occupied again after months of silence since summer. Immersed amidst the trees along its shores, they give the lake a fairy-tale look, reminding us of mysterious northern legends and forest tales, where creatures dance in the snow in the forests. Candles are lit at the entrance to every house and in every garden, moving flames of joy, hope, and welcome. Tapio and Aulikki, the two forest creatures of Finnish tales, move silently behind every trunk and rock, waking the animals and the humans for the Feast of Feasts.

Some candles are lit in ice buckets, made by simply leaving a plastic bucket three quarter full of water outside in the arctic temperature and letting the water freeze. Once it is a solid ice block, the plastic bucket is removed, and what is left is its shape in ice with an empty space in the middle. The block is then turned over and a candle placed in it. As simple as this sounds, the effect of the flickering candle flame seen through the ice is amazing. We asked friends how it was done and tried it ourselves, initially using metal buckets. The result was a broken mess of ice pieces. When friends tell you to use a plastic bucket, that is what you have to do, without arguing the reasoning behind it. We have tried many times since, and it does work. The candles look very nice, and because of the extreme temperature, the candle holders can last a whole winter.

We have sometimes gone for walks on the lake on the dark Christmas Eves, before returning home for a hot and traditional cleansing sauna and then visiting the nearby cemetery, as most Finns do every year, and lighting small candles. The cemetery is on hilly ground, and looking down from the chapel steps, you feel as if a trembling city is at your feet, with its flickering lights shining on every grave, reminding you of the love and respect of the living towards their departed.

On the actual Christmas Day nothing happens on the lake until afternoon, when the effects of the previous evening's food and drink excesses have been slept off. Then skiers get out on the snowy ice for some refreshing and mind-clearing exercise, while less sporty people go for walks in the hope that the lake's freezing winds will blow away the fumes of koskenkorva and vodka.

We keep to our tradition of celebrating Christmas on Christmas Day, delaying our walks on the lake by twenty-four hours. Generally the effects of the roast elk and the joulu kinku (the traditional Christmas ham) go away after a snooze in front of the television, without which Christmas Day would be even more boring.

On a winter's day one of the best views of Paijanne's majestic wilderness is from Tehi. In the Summer Tehi is a kind of bus stop for the passenger boat going from Jyvaskyla to Lahti, and in winter it is simply a wooden jetty stretching over the frozen white surface of the lake. From the end of the jetty the vastness of Paijanne lies in front of you in all its peaceful silence, the immense snow-covered space broken only by the small islands dotted at random in the solid cold desert. You can barely make out the shadow of the coastline by Sysma on the opposite side, some thirty-five kilometres away.

A friend of ours some time ago explained that this long lake is a natural barrier between Finnish characters, with the Savo population to the east – moody, hard, and reserved – and the Kesku and Hame population to the west – more jovial, open, and relaxed. The only experience we have of anyone from the Savo region is a friend who has travelled the world and has lived abroad at length. He is certainly not a reliable example of the alleged character difference, although, in fairness, he on the whole does not like people very much. So something must be true.

We have taken friends and relatives to Tehi, showing them the forest road on the way to Ruolahti, a typical postcard picture image that you see on so many calendars for December, and without exception they have marvelled at Paijanne's natural winter beauty. Despite their different ages, they have all played in the deep snow by the wooden legs of the jetty and have made the famous "snow angels" by lying on the ground and moving their legs and arms in a kind of slow flight. Finland always seems to awaken the child in everyone, with its simple and pure winter environment.

Skidoos are the prevailing vehicles on the frozen Paijanne. I have always looked at them with interest in stores, at times even thinking of buying one. They are impressive, colourful, powerful, and dangerous – potent snow machines that seem to stop at nothing. On the flat surface of the lake they move at terrific speed, lifting clouds of snow powder in their wake, their drivers looking menacing in the dark outfits and helmets. They are all Japanese brands and vary in size, but they are all fast.

Ari came over one day, across Paijanne from his large family home some kilometres away and let me try his skidoo. Only a 250 cc., he told me. Exhilarating and dangerous it was. Unlike a motorbike, it did not bend and tilt to one side upon steering because of the wide snow-gripping belt and the two front skis, as well as its weight and its width. It felt rigid and prone to capsizing, but it was fast and exciting. I went from one side of our corner of Paijanne to the other in a matter of a couple of minutes; in the summer with my rowing boat I take about twenty. Celia has frowned several times at my suggestion that I may need a skidoo. It will have to remain an old man's dream.

The freezing lake in winter also makes it considerably easier to carry out work that would be near impossible on water.

A few years ago we decided that we had had enough of the barrier of reeds by the shoreline. They were tall and dense, and they made it terribly difficult to walk into the water without being bitten almost to death by the millions of aggressive mosquitos hiding in them. In the past we had seen how a house along the coast from us had eliminated its reeds jungle by digging deep into the water with an excavator, lifting the plants from the depth of the lake. The reeds did disappear, but the problem, we recalled, was that for some considerable time the lake water remained very murky and muddy because of the sandy bottom of our section of Paijanne.

We contacted a few people asking for opinions, and someone suggested a system that he had implemented in a number of different places, always with great success and without disrupting the cleanliness of the water for a single moment. We decided to give him a try. He made it very clear that the method had to be used in winter and only if the thickness of the ice was enough to bear the weight of lorries. We were a bit puzzled, but we decided to go along with his plan. It had been a very hard winter, and the temperature had been well below minus 20 Celsius for a long time, so the conditions seemed to be adequate.

The reeds had been dried by the cold and were bent by the snow, blocked in the ice. On the established day, with typical Finnish punctuality, we saw Heikki (a very popular name in Finland) coming across the lake on his huge tractor, carrying some material in the front bucket, which turned out to be an immense sheet of thick felt, the kind used under the layer of tar when roads are made. It was in a roll, and it looked very heavy.

The felt was carefully laid on the whole of the frozen surface of the lake that was affected by the reeds so that it covered a vast area along the shore and several metres into the lake. Our bemusement grew by the minute. Once the job was complete, Heikki sat and waited in the cold. We grew even more puzzled.

After a while a lorry appeared at our gate carrying an enormous amount of sand and started reversing towards the lake shore across the grass. Luckily, the ground was frozen solid after weeks of extreme temperatures, or our garden would have suffered the effect of the weight and shown the tyre marks all through summer.

The sand was unloaded in a big pile over the felt sheet, looking horribly dark against the white snow and ice and Heikki proceeded to spread it evenly with the tractor so that some twenty centimetres of sand were on top of the whole sheet of felt. Twenty centimetres, not one centimetre more or one less, he said. Heikki is an expert at handling a tractor, and the whole job was completed in a reasonably short time despite the vast area involved. In the end, what had been a nice white shoreline now looked like a building site, with brown sand looking strikingly dark against the background of snow and ice on the lake. Heikki and his tractor disappeared across the frozen Paijanne, after assuring us that in spring everything would look perfect. We had no choice but to believe him. We left for England, looking back at the dark sand on our lake and just hoping that Heikki would be proved right.

When we returned in spring, our shore by the lake was a lovely sandy beach, gently sloping into the water, without a single reed in sight. As the ice melted at the end of winter, the weight of the sand had slowly pushed the felt cover down under the water, squashing all the plants and leaving a perfectly clear little bay. How amazingly simple!

The good results of this trick have lasted four years, and only now are we beginning to see some reeds reappear around the edges of what was the felt sheet. The invisible power of the lake waves over the years have pushed and rolled the edges of the felt in all directions so that some of the sandy bottom is once again exposed to the stubbornness of the reeds. All that is needed is another harsh winter and a few more tons of sand, and once again the water will be clear and our view of Paijanne will be completely unobstructed.

During April cracks usually begin to show on the ice, like lines of an ever-expanding web. They slowly let water filter through and soon turn into pools. The ice is pushed against the shores and slowly melted away, with a kind of sizzling noise. The cycle restarts.

Politics

Since its birth as an independent nation free from Sweden and Russia, Finland has been a democracy, and a socialist one too.

It has a President, a prime minister who heads the government, and a Parliament. The basic distribution of the parties can be summed up as left, right, and centre, with coalition governments almost always made up of socialist and centre parties.

It is a simplistic explanation, but, after all, it is like everything else in Finland. There are no complications, and, like work, politics are almost never allowed to interfere with life. The forests are a wonderful safety screen. Politics are not talked about or argued about. Elections come and go, and Finns diligently cast their vote and accept whoever is elected. End of story.

Having lived in Finland for many years now, I can comfortably say that the level of corruption and intrigue within the government is by European standards - let alone by the standards of some countries on other continents - so insignificant that most of the world's communities would jump and dance for joy were their own governments to suffer only from such a weak form of the disease. The thing is that fundamentally Finnish morality is based only on two colours. You pay your bills on time, you keep your word, you obey the rules, and you are good... You try to avoid paying your bills, you evade taxes, you act unreliable, and you are bad. There is no in-between, no acceptable excuse that might distort the truth with some resemblance of justification and reason.

It is a basic and primordial – albeit refreshing – concept in which, if you do wrong, you are punished. Punishment used to consist of chopping off your head, burning you alive on a pile of logs, or offering you to bears for dinner. Finland, being a modern country, now uses as punishment the dismissal or resignation from public offices, exile from your village, or total avoidance of you as an individual.

We have become so accustomed to politicians clinging onto their posts with every tooth – false or otherwise - in their mouth, despite being proven guilty of an offence, be it moral or political in nature, with complete disregard for the meaning of the word "dignity". In fact, in most cases they even become celebrities thanks to their errors, even if during the whole of their political career they had been obscure and insignificant individuals. They never seem to have the courage and the honesty to say sorry and disappear into the oblivion of history.

In Finland such rare people go away, accept their mistakes and shortcomings, and hope that in this way they will be able to maintain face when they meet their neighbours in the supermarket and will have the courage to look straight at them. In life everyone can fail at times. We have been used to corrupt politicians feeling almost proud of having failed and always playing the offended party's theatrical role instead of just disappearing.

It is the same with life in general. Politics in village communities are a world apart from politics in cities. Councillors, who inevitably know almost everyone personally in their districts, try to do their job to the best of their ability, but often they lack the technical knowledge that is required to control and administer modern budgets, with the result that decisions are not taken and things are simply left as they are, generally to the detriment of the village's image and services. They are honest family men who have been appointed to their responsible jobs because of their popularity within the community, but the concept of promoting their village is often completely alien to them. And even though people might grumble silently, no one wishes to upset friends or neighbours by complaining openly.

One amusing example of this is a little expedition with one of our daughter and her husband that we decided to make to something that so often we had seen in the distance across the woods and fields and that had always caught our imagination. It was an old ski-jump tower emerging from the tree tops against the sky, from where – we were told – the view of the forests is stunning.

On a sunny warm day we drove the thirty or so kilometres, until we spotted the tall structure of the ski-jumping facility to the east of us. We followed our sense of direction trying to get close to it. No signs gave us directions or any other information about this vantage point, even though it is actually mentioned in most of the tourist guide books that cover the area.

Finally, we spotted a small wooden signpost and followed the directions, ending on a very stony road that led up a hill, and we finally reached an open space with the towering ski slope on one side, a number of dilapidated old buildings on the other side and wasteland in between. We appeared to be the only ones there and the place had an almost uncomfortable feeling of danger. We looked up at the immensely high concrete structure and wondered.

At one corner of the square base there was an open door that led into a cubicle with a lift and a few leaflets on the walls, trying to promote the place and advertising the nearby famous skiing facility of Himos. We looked at the lift and at its metal door and looked at one another, doubting very much that the contraption was really for public use. On the other hand the leaflets seemed genuine and recent, although we would have felt happier to see some sign of human life as well.

We decided to take the risk and walked into the lift. Pressing the operating button required a great deal of courage and after a long hesitation and a long deep breath we heard the clunking noise as the lift began to move. We stepped out into a small area that must have been the original assembly point for the competing skiers, and still we did not see anyone. Up a couple of ramps of concrete steps we found ourselves in a larger round room with glass on every side, and suddenly the view of the country below was simply stunning. But again nobody was there.

We were walking round when to our surprise a human head suddenly appeared from behind a low desk. A young man was sitting there on a low stool behind an array of leaflets and promotional sheets. "Hello," he said. The situation seemed surreal! We bought some ice cream from him and we asked if he had been busy. He turned out to be a student on a summer job, and he told us that, yes, he had been busy; he had seen about five people that day as well as us four. Busy!

Now, that little story is about a facility that could be exploited and promoted internationally. The panorama from the top is unique and the surrounding countryside beautiful, and yet the local council has opted to let the tower go into dilapidation, with its jumping slope made up of wooden slats now breaking up and rotting. There is no proper advertising that might attract visitors who could bring income, and there is apparently no intention to clear the wasteland down below. The situation is just deplorable. And nobody seems to mention it or complain or ask the council to resign. This is not an isolated example, but Finns do not complain.

The European Union has in a way helped stimulate the interest of the population towards politics, simply because the most unpopular decisions can now be attributed to Brussels, and very often with good reason. Like the re-introduction of wolves in the forests, regulations about the size and shape of bananas, and the imminent prohibition of terva as a roof cover for old buildings and churches. The decisions are frowned upon, discussed, criticised for a few minutes, and then they are pragmatically accepted in the light of the fact that the Finnish government has approved them.

I remember when Finland finally joined the European Union and soon after that changed its currency from the old Markka to the Euro. The historic decision was applauded by a population who, after centuries of balancing between East and West and of decades of looking with anxiety at its Russian neighbour, felt that the isolation had ended. Finland was now part of the western world and of a fast growing economy that promised to be larger than the world itself...

Everything happened smoothly and the transition from Markka to Euro took place without trauma; the two currencies ran in parallel for a while and then became one. Shoppers of all ages received comprehensive information and help, and almost overnight they became accustomed to recognizing the newly introduced coins and notes. I have to admit that I was amazed at how simply elderly people, coming to the village to shop from their log houses in the forest, mastered the new money without hesitation and with a confidence that put us at shame. It was all a question of acceptance of the government's announcement. The government is the elected body of representatives chosen by the people to preserve and promote the interests of the nation. It is inconceivable not to listen to them or not to trust them. They are Finns.

Brussels is another story.

The issue of the wolves has raised not one but many eyebrows. The EU civil servants in their wisdom decided that not only should Finland have its share of immigrants and people who were politically threatened in their own countries and "demanding" asylum, it should also help the environment by releasing into the wild packs of wolves, so as to return nature to its original habitat. This time the wolves did not come from Russia but from Brussels. They are now a protected species, whilst dogs and other animals, as well as children, do not have to be protected from them. I have heard that after a series of attacks on pets and after several viewings of wolves happily roaming village roads, in certain parts of the country the wolf's population has suddenly diminished. Apparently, it is easy to mistake a wolf for an elk in the twilight in the forest, and the mistake is of course always noticed when it is far too late for the wolf. What a great pity. I said that Finns are always pragmatic.

The terva subject is also a questionable decision taken in Brussels. Terva is a tarry material that for centuries has been used to cover the wooden tiles of both house and church roofs. It gives a beautiful black shiny look to the roofs, it is waterproof, and it smells healthy. When I was a child I remember at times taking some cough sweets that smelt like terva, and the common opinion was that they were good for soothing the cough and the lungs. I also remember watching those huge machines that laid half the road surface in no time by dropping and flattening tons of tar; the steaming black compound smelt like terva.

When summers are very hot – and they can be very hot even in Finland – the terva melts and runs along the gradients of the roofs and is collected in containers strategically placed at the corners of buildings to be used again. I do not think anyone has died from the fumes of terva, although I have no statistical data at hand.

Suddenly Brussels decided that terva can no longer be used, a diktat that has raised several eyebrows. The bureaucrats decided that the tar content in the terva might be a fire hazard, despite the fact that for centuries terva has been the traditional roof cover and sealant on most churches.

As if Brussels had no more serious matters to debate and ponder about! But once again the new regulations will be implemented by the Finns with stoical obedience. It is a reflection of their inborn respect for authority and particularly for the Finnish authority that, after all, debated the terva question in the European Parliament and democratically accepted the verdict.

We have been through two presidential elections and two general elections in Finland.

Mrs Tarja Halonen took over from Mr Matti Arti-Sari, who is now one of the most respected statesmen on the world scene, and she is still the president at the time of writing this book. The elections took place in an air of calm and tranquillity that is typical of Finland. A few boards were put up in the village, showing images of the candidates. There was some TV coverage, in which reporters tried to stimulate debates. And nothing more.

The general elections did not make much more noise. Calendars showed that Election Day was to be a Flag Day, one of the occasions when if you have a flag pole in your garden you fly the white and blue national flag. They came and went with no disruptions, and the few banners disappeared without even leaving bits of paper on the ground. The new government was elected, and it was not very different from the previous one, which after all was rather satisfactory anyway. These governments were coalitions.

You cannot but realize that in this country the politicians and the press have a much higher opinion of their own audiences than in most other nations, where people are generally treated with a contempt that verges on arrogance and disdain and are subsequently ignored anyway. Finland being so small in numbers makes it still

possible for individuals to point fingers and find accountability. Politicians do not live in their ethereal paradises, disconnected from the reality of the country, untouchable and above reproach. Here they have summer cottages by lakes and in small villages, where they can be seen and talked to and looked at straight in their eyes.

On that summer day, when we went to Veikko's farmhouse to celebrate with many other of his friends his sixtieth birthday, we had a little lunch in an old cowshed that had been cleaned and polished and adorned by local girls. At one of the impromptu tables a cabinet Minister was enjoying the simple lunch with his wife. He was an old school friend of Veikko's. He was there, sitting on benches in the concrete environment that had accommodated farm animals in the past, just one of the many guests in the middle of the forest.

Strangely enough, despite the past history of the relationship between Russia and Finland, some left-wing sympathisers do exist and have a presence in the government. They are of communist tendencies but with a touch of Finnish colour. They hold no extreme political belief that makes them very different from other political parties. After all, the country is economically sound, technologically advanced, recognized and respected on the world scene and full of common sense. In this global financial environment, where businesses of all kinds are intermingled and tied by invisible but tangible umbilical cords, financial problems do occur as an inevitable reflection of the markets round the planet. Opposition, if exercised in a constructive manner, can only be a useful and positive factor to keep the ruling parties on their toes and the Finnish Left is the expression of the pragmatism that is prevailing in this country. The nation's interest always come first for real, and meeting in the middle is generally the solution – to everyone's benefit in true democratic fashion.

Handymen

Once we had to call an electrician. Some work was needed in the main fuse box that controlled the whole of the electricity supply to the house. I can just about change a light bulb or install a set of Christmas lights, but not much more. (These lights are always put into storage after working perfectly for the whole of a Christmas festive period and then rolled up around logs so as not to entangle the leads or break the small filaments, but when the following Christmas they are carefully unpacked and placed on the tree, there always seem to be a few that do not work.) This is especially true in view of the present EU legislation that dictates that every bit of electrical work requires a properly approved and baptized electrician, who then has to issue a "certificate of certification".

The electrician who had been introduced to us in the past goes by the name of Tapio (once again, the creature of the forests), but he is universally and affectionately known as Tapsa. He lives not too far from us. He is a very pleasant man with a grey beard not dissimilar to mine, who speaks exceptionally good English, having learnt it by watching and listening to British TV programs.

Tapsa came to see us rather late at night, in the freezing cold, and inspected the fuse box outside the house. He also came in (probably to warm himself up a little) and tested the fuses in the indoor box. He changed one of the large fuses by the garage that apparently did not have the right level of power or resistance and the problem was resolved.

"How much do I owe you, Tapsa?" Five euro was the answer. Yes, five Euro.

Tapsa has been back to our place many times for various reasons: a new electrical central-heating system, new sockets, new wiring, a sensor for the garden lights, and so on. Sometimes he has charged us the above five Euro, other times larger and more realistic amounts. Often he was left on his own in the house to carry on with the jobs whilst we went back to England, for us only to return to completed work and to a clean house.

The call-out charge to which we have been so accustomed in England seems something that has not yet reached Finnish shores. In the village Tapsa is happy with his customers and wants to keep them. He meets them regularly, bumping into them in supermarkets, in the hardware store, in the florist or in a bar. He knows that charging fifty or even one hundred Euro for a small job today may mean no Euro tomorrow and dirty looks in the street. He also knows that five Euros today might not cover the cost of petrol to visit a customer or the cost of a hot drink to warm up after inspecting fuses in sub-zero temperatures, but they may mean much more profitable work tomorrow.

I said that Finns are pragmatic.

The very first time Tapsa came to our house (for reasons that I forget), he would not speak English. He was rather reserved and seemed to rely on the translation that Harri the plumber could arrange in order to understand exactly what we needed. That was until Celia looked at him and asked him straight out if the work we required was difficult. "A piece of cake," came Tapsa's reply, given with a twinkle in his eye.

Since then Tapsa's shyness has gone, and he has helped us out of many situations requiring electrical expertise. Now he converses with us in his astonishing self-taught English. Sometimes he still charges us the traditional five euro and has a beer in the kitchen with me.

I remember once mentioning to Tapsa the idea of having an outdoor electric socket for some extra garden lights that would make the whole place look exotic on winter evenings, together with some new lights of the mushroom type, only a few inches tall and fashionable. Tapsa smiled at our naivety. The lights we were suggesting would be completely covered by snow in winter, and the socket that we had in mind, low on the wall, would be against the law and would be a hazard once under snow. We blushed and decided to go for lights over a metre tall and for sockets that are almost at eye level. Finland is really different.

Harri is another example. Tall, blond, strong, and a rally driver, he is the village plumber. Together with Seppo, the car mechanic, he has a history of taking part in rally competitions.

Plumbing is rather peculiar in Finland. All pipes are hidden and never seem to freeze, even at minus 40 Celsius. We asked Harri to install an outside tap at the back of our house so that I could water the plants and wash the car without having to drag behind me some eighty metres of hose (that always gets kinks in the farthest end and makes you constantly mad, standing there holding the nozzle and looking miserably at the few drops leaking out).

Harri came, punctual like everyone else in this country, and worked for about forty-five minutes, drilling a hole through the shower room and connecting the cold water pipe to a tap that he placed on the outside wall. Once the work was completed, Harri gave us some advice as to how to turn the tap off correctly, so that no water would remain in the pipe after we had used the hose.

The tap outside our house is a normal steel tap, receiving water from the main supply that also feeds the shower room washbasin taps indoors. Since installing it, we have been to almost minus 40 Celsius for prolonged periods during winters, but mysteriously enough the tap has never frozen. This is probably because the pipes bringing the water to the house are very deep in the ground and because the log structure of the house acts as insulator. Whatever the reason or mechanical explanation, our taps and pipes have never frozen in all the winters we have spent in Finland. Comparisons with poor old England, where everything freezes as soon as temperatures reach zero, are inevitable – and embarrassing.

Water is another element with which I prefer not to play. In Milan when Celia and I were first married and lived in a dainty small apartment, one evening I decided that I could fix a gas water heater on the wall over our bath. The experiment ended with me standing with my feet on either side of the bath holding an umbrella, trying without success to stop the cold water gushing out of the dreadful apparatus. We had to call an expert.

I remember once when Harri had to do some rather menial job. He was with us for about twenty minutes, and at the end came the usual question, "Harri, how much do I owe you?" Five Euros was the reply. I have no idea whether Tapsa and Harri had plotted together to charge us only five Euro for small jobs. I began to develop the thought that all small electric and plumbing jobs in Finland were always five Euros.

Harri comes every Autumn to our place – when we are generally in England – and, knowing all our secrets, he lets himself into the garden sauna to disconnect and remove the pump that he installed years ago for us to have running water from the lake. The pump is then stored in his warm garage through winter and put back into place in spring, ready for use when the lake is not frozen. He is efficient, reliable, and honest. What more do we want?

It was not easy at first. We were not familiar with local people, and the language barrier was a serious impediment for us to explain what was needed either inside or outside the house. We had to rely on advice from our few initial acquaintances who suggested this or that carpenter, or roofer, or general handyman. Also, we were still strange people from abroad, inspiring a certain amount of shyness and doubt, and we always seemed to be put at the end of the priority list. The general impression was that everyone was too busy even to give us an idea of when the work (big or small) could be carried out. The answer to our usual question "When?" tended to be always, "I do not know … am busy … maybe next month … ehka … .maybe." Ehka is one of the Finns' favourite expressions. It gives them time to think and not commit themselves to dates. Everyone loves their "maybe".

Many years ago we met a couple of friends who had just moved into a house near the village centre. We were told that they were trying to buy it, as it was comfortable, convenient for the village shopping, and large enough to accommodate the whole family as well as to hold parties for their teenage sons and daughter. An offer had apparently been submitted to the house owner. When we raised the inevitable question, "When do you think you will buy it?" the answer was just as inevitable: "Maybe next month ... ehka." They did buy it the following month.

Once we became more regular and established faces around the village and people began to believe that, after all, we were not going to bite them and we were going to pay our bills, the situation dramatically improved. Now I can certainly say that we are surrounded by excellent handymen who seem to take a great interest in helping us and whose expertise we can totally rely upon.

Finns are reserved and slow to open up to newcomers, but when they finally do so they open up wholeheartedly and sincerely – as long as you never let them down.

Taxis

For many inhabitants of the Finnish forests taxis are the only mean of transport that allows them to go to the villages and buy provisions. There is, of course, an excellent public transport system, with buses reaching even remote communities and running on narrow and perilous roads that would be generally suited only for elks. All the same, it cannot be expected that buses should stop at every household that has a colourful post box at the top of the lane.

So taxies are the solution, and taxi drivers become welcome friendly faces to many. In some cases, especially the elderly who live alone and isolated, they may be the only faces that they see from time to time. Drivers become helpful and trusted companions. We often see taxis in the village parked outside a supermarket or the chemist, waiting for their old and regular customers to finish shopping. The driver will load the bags and sometimes wheelchairs – into the car boot and will return the customers to their forest homes, feeling happier for having enjoyed a little social life.

A few years ago someone told us that one particular driver in the village, who regularly transported an old lady to her usual supermarket or to her doctor or to the chemist, noticed that his passenger on her shopping expeditions was buying ever-growing quantities of bottled water and appeared constantly tired. The lady was living alone and very seldom had visitors who would justify the large consumption of water.

The driver took it upon himself to contact one of the lady's distant relatives who had moved a long way up north and was now rarely in touch with the ageing woman. He expressed his concern at what appeared to him as a sudden surge in thirst, even when weather conditions were far from hot and dry. The distant relative decided to visit the elderly lady and have her inspected by a doctor. It turned out that she was suffering from diabetes, something that had never been detected and had never caused alarm. This lady is still alive to this day, taking medications and still enjoying her taxi trips to the village. The driver may have saved her life.

One winter we became very ill with an unpleasant flu bug that confined both of us to bed for a few days feeling like death. We could not go out, we had no energy left in our limbs, and we thought the end had come. Finally, on a Saturday of all days, I decided to call a doctor friend of ours, asking him for some advice as to how we could find a local doctor who would come and see us. Our friend asked about our symptoms and decided to telephone the local chemist in his medical capacity, ordering some antibiotics for us and requesting the chemist to arrange for a taxi to deliver them to our home. No more than an hour later a taxi driver was at the door with the prescription medicine. I paid the amount that he mentioned, and we were cured. I like to say that our friend and that taxi driver practically saved our lives. When a few days later I walked into the chemist wishing to pay for the antibiotics, I was informed that the taxi driver had paid for them and just added the cost to his own bill. Everything had been sorted out.

You become affectionate and familiar with taxi drivers. You confide in them and are disappointed when you are told that they are on holiday – almost questioning the fact that they are entitled to breaks too.

When Celia was left alone in Finland a couple of times, very much at the beginning of our Finnish adventure, she had to use taxis to go everywhere. She can drive and has had for many years a British driving licence which has never had any penalty points on it. She used to drive extremely well and had her own sports car, which she often pushed to the limit of its speed with competence. Many years ago she suddenly lost her confidence and decided that driving was no longer for her. Driving had become a worrying burden for her on the congested English roads, and she gave up her beloved car. She has never driven since, with one or two rare exceptions in Finland (where roads are empty anyway); she would drive on the small lane leading to our forest cottage, where the only encounter might be a lost elk in search of his mum or a sparrow hawk hovering in search of a mouse or a young rabbit.

So Celia depended on taxis.

One day she came across Markku, one of the small group of drivers who are based in a tiny office in the village, from which they respond to calls. Markku was unknown to Celia; simply one of the taxis. Driving is his business, and he seems to be busy all the time, being a popular figure in the community. When he is not in his taxi, he often relaxes by going for long motorcycle journeys across the country with his wife. In winter he becomes a great skidoo expert and enthusiast, often mapping the usable tracks through the forests for skidoo drivers.

Celia was taken to the village supermarket, and once they were back at our place, Markku helped her unload her shopping. It was still the time when the Finnish language was completely unfamiliar to us, and Celia tried her hardest to thank Markku in Finnish, managing only to say "Good Morning" several times while wanting to thank him! It has never been forgotten.

We have become friends with Markku and his wife, despite the fact that we have always made a clear distinction between personal and business affairs. Whenever we arrive at Vantaa airport, Markku's friendly face is there to meet us and give us the first welcome to Finland. He is a tall gentle man, with a slight paunch, probably due to some past beer enjoyment. He is besotted with his grandchild Susanna, proud of his home and family, and dedicated to his great passions, skidoo trekking through forests and motorbikes.

Apart from a limited number of social encounters, we see Markku only when we arrive at Helsinki airport or leave home to fly back to England. Even with our – albeit limited – improvement in mastering the Finnish language, our conversations with Markku generally exhaust all subjects and all words we know after only ten or so kilometres from home, and the remaining two hours of the journey to Vantaa are always consumed in complete silence, interrupted only by Celia occasionally offering a round of sweets. I am sure that we must be the most boring customers that Markku has ever had in his entire taxiing career.

On arrival, we are always tired from the journey from London and from the very early morning awakening that ensured there would be no delays in reaching Heathrow airport. As a result, soon after leaving Vantaa we both snooze off, and almost every time we only wake up when we are about half an hour from home. I am also sure that when Markku receives a call on his mobile telephone while driving us, it must be one of his friends whom he asked to call him between our village and Vantaa so as to remind him that there are still living people on our planet. But he is always there to meet us when we arrive, smiling and warm. We feel we have arrived in Finland.

And he is always the last face we see from our village when we go through the automatic doors at Vantaa, pushing our trolley towards the airline desks for our return to England.

Next time Markku will be there again to welcome us. And there will be many more times. Finland is now in our blood; and it is there to stay.

About the Author

British by nationality but born and educated in Italy, the author has spent most of his adult life in England, although his international marketing business has taken him to many parts of the world and has allowed him to develop the ability to understand and respect different cultures.

After a number of works written and published on the subject of international business, this is the author's first attempt at a book aimed at the general readership.

He lives with his wife in England and Finland.

Lightning Source UK Ltd.
Milton Keynes UK
UKOW051254280312

189761UK00002B/24/P